Charlie Hardie

The Black Raven:
Those Who Suffered Under Communism

By
Charles Hardie

ISBN: 1-4196-7786-1

ISBN-13: 978-1419677861

Visit www.booksurge.com to order additional copies.

RETURN TO DEEP CREEK BAPTIST CHURCH

DEDICATION

This book is humbly dedicated to the individuals who lost their lives at the hands of deceived murderers. Those dear ones did not have a chance to tell their stories. I respectfully dedicate this book to their memories.

ACKNOWLEDGEMENT

To my wife Phyllis, I thank you for your patience with me while writing this book.

To my interpreters and hosts, I give great credit to all of you for putting up with me as I worked on collecting these stories. These individuals are Victor and Larisa Kumskov, Albina, Erina Vlasenka, Katia, Yuri, Anya, Peter, Ola, Luda and Zenia. Thank you!

To the large number of friends who helped me record the interviews, I am deeply thankful to all of you.

Special thanks goes to Erina Vlasenka who helped me the most in both 2005 and 2006. She made numerous telephone calls and arranged interviews for me. In addition, Erina helped me interpret the interviews from the cassette tapes.

I will always be grateful to my dear friend, Reverend Ben Tomlinson, who was the first one to read this book. Thanks so much, Ben.

Dr. Waylon B Moore, founder and CEO of Missions Unlimited, Inc gave encouragement and his endorsement. Thanks so much Waylon for your very kind words.

To my good missionary friend and counselor, Dr. Steve Hunter, thank you for taking time from your busy schedule as a professor at Criswell College to read my book. Steve, you and Karen are the best.

One other very long-time friend is John Walcott, owner of Walcott Studio. John, thanks so much for giving your time and energy to prepare the images for this book. Our friendship continues.

Last, and most important of all, is Tui Bedwell, daughter of John Walcott, who labored long and hard over the proofreading and many, many suggestions for this book. Apart from her labor of love, dear reader, you would not have this document before you.

AUTHOR'S NOTE

Due to security reasons, I changed one name in the book. I want to apologize in advance for any mistakes in names or places. I know how important it is for me to get everything perfect when it is written down. It is the Russian way of doing things, especially when preparing documents. I fear however, that I have made some mistakes. Yet, at the same time, I have worked hard to be very accurate.

People who are still alive, or have passed away since I interviewed them, tell the personal stories in this book. Yet, other stories come from loved ones who lost their relatives. No matter who told the story, it is important for us to hear about these true heroes.

These heroes died in many different ways, but had a few things in common. Their bodies were diseased, filled with pain and malnourished. Family members did not hear their final words. In addition, life was void of music, doctors and healthcare professionals, medicine, food, drink and a proper burial with flowers and a casket. This was the life, and ultimate death, of a Russian prisoner.

The arrested individuals, and even their families, became known as an 'enemy of the people.' To whom (the communists, Joseph Stalin), life was very, very cheap and meant very little. Even the guard dogs were fed better and more valuable than the prisoners. Most of society was struggling to hold onto life. With these conditions, how could people show sympathy to those in their final moments?

CONTENTS

Vicelly Simonovich

Nicolai and Nina Zezula

Pavel Merkoulovitch

Yakov Feuderovich

Annya at the Razavet Church

Victor Vacillovich at the Razavet Church

Alexei Iznatchevich in Pestila

Sergei the Prisoner

Mehaill Porhornovich Strelkov

Maria at the Razavet Church

Stalin's Spy

Stories from the Ukraine and Belorussia

Nadezhda and her Family

Maria Zaharchenko in Mariupol

Vladimir Vilchinsky

INTRODUCTION

Why another book on the sufferings of the Russian people when there are already so many on this subject? It is because there is no end to the stories about this vast land and the depth of suffering these people have endured. My wife Phyllis and I served more than nine years in Siberia as Baptist missionaries. We wanted to tell the stories of individuals with whom we had contact and how their lives have affected our lives. One cannot live in a country for such an extended period and not get a feel for the culture.

Before I begin, I must explain the division of Russia. Within this country, there are numerous oblasts, six krais and about 12 republics. Oblasts are smaller regions and krais are larger regions. Republics are similar to states but they are unique because they have their own governors. Russian soldiers live here to maintain the connection between Moscow and the republic.

The contrast between the philosophy of Russia and America has often astounded me. To me, the American dream describes our attitude toward life. "Make it as comfortable, effective and efficient as possible with a minimum of effort and difficulty." The Russian concept in the days of Joseph Stalin was one word, "suffering." One day Stalin took a live chicken and plucked off all of its feathers. This left the creature without protection from the cold. As a result, the chicken leaned up against him to stay warm. He said, "This is what I do to my people."

My question to God is, "How can I possibly communicate what I saw and felt as I listened to the many interviews of these dear people?" They shared with me their stories of the unbelievable pain and sufferings they endured during those very difficult times. My deep cry is, "Dear God, please help me with this monumental task for you."

In the early 1990's, Russia's economy was having difficulty moving from a centrally controlled economy to a more open market economy. It appeared that life would be more comfortable in the future. However, when a building in Moscow was blown up, and people were killed, a woman said, "Now I feel like a Russian." At that time, I had difficulty understanding what she meant. As we lived in Russia, and had trouble with some of these same things, Phyllis and I understood more fully what this woman meant.

Why the title *Black Raven?* The KGB, previously known as the NKVD, carried out most of the arrests in Russia. This means that the NKVD, KGB and the *Black Raven* are synonymous. These men wore black coats, arrived in a black van, and would usually make their arrests between 3 and 5 a.m. The Russian people called this black van the *Black Raven*. It was a feared vehicle that came to many homes and took away mainly fathers and husbands. The final destination of the arrested men was the commandant, the prison and for many, death. Most of the children in these homes would awake to discover their mother weeping over the loss of their father who was the financial provider for the family. For those families, it was a time of great stress.

On June 20, 1993, my wife Phyllis, and I arrived in Russia. Upon our arrival, we noticed that most of the people were not smiling. They also did not seem to want us in their country. There were, however, a few believers living in Russia and they seemed to be grateful to have us there.

We knew we had a lot to learn about our new life in Russia. The exchange rate was just one of those lessons. One day we took a taxi from the restaurant back to our hotel in Moscow. At the end of our ride, we mistakenly paid the taxi driver $23 instead of $3. Another learning experience occurred on the train. After a few days of orientation in Moscow, we packed some food and took the Trans Siberian rail to our new mission field. THE TRIP TOOK US 53 HOURS! It was a lot of rocking and rolling, but we made it in good shape. Some men from the Baptist church picked us up in the church's old van and took us to an apartment in southwest Novosibirsk. As we settled into our new surroundings, we continued to discover that virtually no one smiled.

In October 1993, during the attempted coup to oust President Boris Yeltsin, we were staying in a hotel in Moscow. We were told to stay out of sight, keep all of the blinds pulled and only turn on the toilet light. We were under hotel arrest for 36 hours. There was virtually no food in the hotel. Some visiting missionaries from Kentucky let us share some food that they had brought with them. That night, we saw and heard the tracer bullets going toward the TV tower located in a field across the street. When we first heard the sound of shots, we were reminded of the firecrackers that are so prevalent in Taiwan at weddings and other events.

Later that month, we traveled back to Novosibirsk, which was another 53-hour ride. This time we carried with us footlockers containing canned food. The train's conductress was very angry that we "dumb Americans" were trying to sneak heavy containers on board without paying for the excess baggage. Our translator did not think it would be a problem. The conductress strongly considered not letting us board the train. At the last minute, she reluctantly permitted us to board. Her loud remarks continued even after we boarded the train. We did not fully understand, except we knew that her remarks had to do with our baggage and money. I gave her all of my small change, about $11 American dollars, and offered her my rubles. She refused, saying that the rubles were only tokens. I will never forget her Russian word. It was "*kopecky.*" We were under a lot of pressure during this train ride. The conductress even threatened to take Phyllis's coat, but my wife would not allow it. In fact, Phyllis was tempted to try out the strength of her new mop over her head. Nevertheless, wisdom prevailed and a bigger scene was averted. Finally, a dear man and professor from one of the Novosibirsk universities who spoke some broken English talked with the conductress and she finally left. After this incident, be assured we kept a very low profile for the long ride to Novosibirsk, a city of about 1.3 million people in south-central Russia. As we departed this dear train conductress, I gave her an Eternal Life tract that she took reluctantly. It was easy to notice she was an alcoholic. We truly rejoiced when the train arrived in our new adopted city with the canned food intact. Because food was scarce, we thoroughly enjoyed that food.

The first apartment we lived in did not have a telephone, so we used public phones. Phyllis's birthday is July 4. This was our fifth day in Novosibirsk. We were able to go to the local hotel and call our girls to let them know where we were. The call lasted 10 minutes and it cost $40 after the operator had gotten our girls on the line. We were experiencing a heavy adjusting curve. After this and other experiences, we found ourselves evaluating our future years here in Russia. We asked this question, "Dear God, what have we gotten ourselves into in this voluntary exile?"

As you read this book, I leave you with this question. Are cultures different? As missionaries in Taiwan, we adjusted without a lot of difficulty; however, in Russia, we found our motto "not wrong; just different" to be tested to the limit.

Section I

STORIES FROM WESTERN NOVOSIBIRSK COUNTY

Demetri and Lyudmilla

It was a snowy, overcast day in March 2006 as Alexei and I put on our boots, wool scarves, fur lined hats, leather coats and gloves. We walked from Alexei's 5-room apartment down the hill to the bus stop in Novosibirsk. In my hands was a very small bag with enough clothing and toiletries to sustain me for only three days. I also took with me my trusty old tape recorder, transformer and audiocassettes; items I never forget when traveling.

My host, Erina Vlasenka, made all of my travel arrangements. Erina was one of my original Russian tutors. In 1993, she started tutoring me. Since then, she has become one of our very best friends in Russia. Her English is impeccable. She is very kind and cooperative in every way. Moreover, she is a radiant Christian and has a wonderful family.

I strongly resisted being escorted to the Novosibirsk train station since I felt I was an experienced traveler in Siberia. Nevertheless, Alexei insisted he escort me. We took a taxi van, paid 10 rubles per person and within about 25 minutes arrived at the train station. He escorted me inside, asked for track number three, we said our goodbyes and I boarded the Silver Eagle. My final destination was a small town west of Novosibirsk, Tatarsk. It was here I would meet Demetri, a Baptist pastor.

As soon as I stepped off the train in Tatarsk, Demetri started toward me. We greeted one another by removing our gloves. This is the respectable thing to do regardless of the weather. Upon our meeting, we immediately departed by foot for his church building named 'Prayer House.' This is where he and Lyudmilla, his wife, lived. As we walked, I noticed the wind was fierce. It reminded me again, how poorly I had packed my clothing for this trip. After a short 15-minute walk, we arrived at this quaint little Baptist church of Tatarsk, nestled in the western side of this small town of 25,000 people.

This small church was nicely painted white with green shutters. Its auditorium contained straight chairs for worship and was about 20 feet X 30 feet. The kitchen was 10 feet by 20 feet and was used for many purposes: the kitchen, living room, bedroom, bathroom and dining room. Outside of the kitchen were an inner corridor and an outer corridor, both of which were very small. Incidentally, the outer corridors were used to trap the bitter cold from coming into the house as individuals enter and leave.

While shaving at the sink, located in the corner of the kitchen, the next morning, Lyudmilla pulled a privacy curtain behind me. Both Demetri and Lyudmilla thoroughly enjoy this modified living area and made it very comfortable for themselves. I admire their simple living style. They did not feel deprived at all.

Demetri asked me if I wanted to see the Fifty-Day Church and meet a fellow-believer named Sergei. The Fifty-Day Church was the Pentecostal church. After I finally understood Demetri's question, I energetically agreed. As we walked in the fierce winds, I was reminded of the winds in western Texas or Oklahoma. The only difference was it was much colder here. We went to the second floor of the church and met an older gentleman named Sergei, who welcomed us heartily. His very small apartment was clean and neat. Demetri explained the purpose of our visit to Sergei. He agreed to give us an interview and I immediately began setting up my recording equipment. Sergei spoke very slowly, which revealed his mind did not function as quickly as it used to. I also noticed he had characteristics found in someone with a Chinese background. He confirmed this suspicion when he shared that his family members were Buddhists. Sergei accompanied us to the outside door. This gesture is very characteristic of Chinese people, but is not exclusive to it. You will read about the story of Sergei from Tatarsk in the next section.

As we started walking back toward Demetri's home, the brightly shining Siberian sun beamed down upon us, which helped against the bitter wind. We walked 45 minutes before arriving at his home. Along the way, we met a church member and her young son. Demetri told me this woman had just ended her habit of alcoholism.

She was joyful to see her pastor. As we all talked, I frequently shifted my bag from one hand to the other. By doing this, I managed to keep one hand in my leather jacket pocket and avoid excessive cold on my hands. The gloves I borrowed from my host family were not designed to keep out the cold. During those moments, I deeply regretted not remembering to bring this significant item. I wish that knowledge meant obedience; but many times, I have known better but have not done better.

At about 1:30 p.m., Lyudmilla called Demetri on his cellular telephone concerned about our tardiness. He assured her we were walking at a steady pace toward their home. Upon our arrival, we sat down to a very good meal. Our first entrée was soup. It was hot and delicious. This side dish was then followed with meatballs, two kinds of bread, Lyudmilla's homemade cheese, homemade honey for our hot tea, pickles for our meat and rice. In addition, for dessert, we had a bar of chocolate. Lunch concluded with a second prayer. It is customary for Russian Baptists to pray both before and after their meals. The meal was very special and it felt good to sit and visit.

During the afternoon, I continued reading Aleksandr Solzhenitsyn's book on the Archipelago. This book describes the gulags, the horrible prison camps of Russia and gives many insights into Siberia. While I was reading, Lyudmilla brought in a very unusual heater for my feet. It was a 2-foot by 3-foot flat and thin board. It had wires in it that connected to an outlet. The heater worked fine and did not get too hot. While I continued reading, Lyudmilla sat it in a chair opposite my feet. I enjoyed my reading in their small auditorium. That night I slept on a bed constructed of straight chairs put together with a thick blanket over them. It was quite comfortable and I slept well. In the morning, I awoke ready for the day's work.

The time I spent with Demetri and Lyudmilla was very enjoyable. Numerous times I was reminded of how these two were humble servants trying to win their small city to our Savior.

Sergei from Tatarsk

I met Sergei during the time I spent with Demetri and Lyudmilla. He was the pastor of the Pentecostal Church in Tatarsk. Here is the story of what his life was like growing up in Russia.

He was born on the River Volga, located south of Moscow in the Astrakhanskaya Oblast. Sergei's parents were fishermen. After some time, his family moved to Azerbaijan. It was after this move that his father died. Sergei's mother was too poor to care for the children. This meant Sergei and his three sisters would live as orphans in an orphanage. A few years later, one sister got married and was able to be free from the orphanage. Sergei was the youngest of the four children. He was uneducated and had no one to raise him or give him ideas.

Life was very, very difficult while Sergei was growing up. His family had no money for school supplies or clothes. They did have one cow; however, the government required everyone to give 200 liters of milk as a tax to support the war. Families were also required to give eggs, vegetables and meat to the government. They were also required to give a hog or bull if it could be slaughtered. These living conditions and governmental requirements continued until the war ended.

During WWII, Sergei was sent to study in the university. Instead, he enlisted in the army and studied in a military school. At the completion of military school, he was given the rank of lieutenant before he went to war. While at war, he received a message stating his mother was being sent to Siberia. The letter read, "Do not come home because she will not be there." After the war, he returned home and became a believer.

One night, in the very early morning hours, there was a knock on his door. It was the NKVD (*Black Raven*) coming to arrest him. In those days, believers were thought to be 'enemies of the people.' It was believed that these individuals had to be punished and reeducated. Sergei was exiled to a camp in the northern Krasnoyarsk Region and was asked why he had chosen religion. The official reason he was exiled was his papers were not in order. It was common for problems to occur with an individual's documents. These problems gave government officials an excuse to send people to camp. Camp was a place of exile for prisoners and not reeducation. The reality was the Russian government had two purposes for exile. The first was death through unreasonable, inhuman work and very little food. The second was free labor.

Winters in Krasnoyarsk were very cold. At times, the night temperatures dropped to negative 60 degrees. Sergei had only one cotton-padded, worn coat. He did not have any gloves because those were not given to prisoners. His job at the camp was to help cut the huge trees that would be floated down the river to be processed in another region. If the river were frozen, the logs would be stored on the riverbank and floated down it after the thaw in May. If the prisoners did not reach their daily quota, they would not receive their slice of bread and hot watery soup for supper. Sergei also mentioned it was common to see prisoners eating grass to stay alive.

At the end of each day, the prisoners fell into their wooden bunks totally exhausted. They were given a few ragged blankets to help keep warm. If they used their cotton-padded coats as quilts, they were beaten. During the summer, the gnats and mosquitoes were so thick that the workers had to constantly fight them off just to have a slight measure of sanity. What the prisoners really needed was a wire net around for their heads to keep off the insects.

After several years, Sergei was released from the camp. He was then arrested again. This time he was tried for being a believer and sent to prison. The NKVD (*Black Raven*) accused him of stealing, but he told them he was not a criminal. He was advised to say nothing. The authorities asked him why he was silent. He said, "I don't want you to use my words against me." The authorities put him in prison and told the other prisoners he was the most dangerous prisoner there. Because of this, he was not accepted in the prison, he was labeled an 'enemy of the people' and had to live in a hut.

Finally, after ten years, Sergei was released from prison. He traveled from village to village trying to find a place to stay but no one received him. It was because the people feared the law that said, "If you help an 'enemy of the people,' you yourself are an enemy." Sergei did not believe this law. He believed, "God never abandoned me."

It was now 1952 or 1953. Stalin was still alive and Sergei continued his ministry by becoming a pastor. He was able to save a little bit of money after his time in prison. With this money, he purchased a small house and then the blessings began to flow. God gave him a Christian wife, a son and a large number of Christian friends. After an unknown amount of time, his wife, son and brother all died. Most deaths during this time were a result of poor healthcare and a poor diet. "Death was very common in those days," said Sergei. He spent 20 years serving as a Pentecostal pastor to 30 to 50 believers. Currently, that number is less. Another brother in Christ now leads the church. Sergei feels this man is not a very mature leader and God is not too pleased; however, God does look upon the heart.

We do not know what tomorrow holds but we do know who holds our tomorrow. Everything is from God and a time will come when Sergei will die. Before that time comes, he does not want to be paralyzed or in bed for a long time because there is no one to care for him. Sergei said this because he knew a woman in his church that was paralyzed and in bed for five years.

As I sat at the feet of this dear saint, who is waiting for his name to be called in heaven, my heart was moved. I realized again, here is a brother who stayed true to the father and did not fail to carry out God's will for his life. His strong faith and determination brought him through all of the inhuman treatments he received at the hands of a deceived people. Sergei understood that only his faith could have sustained him in the forest when the communists tried to starve him and work him to death.

Currently, Sergei is living in a one-room apartment that was given to him. It has a toilet and bath next door. This was truly an act of God's mercy. He is very pleased with it and feels very unworthy to receive it. He has experienced many hard times in life, but now his life is much easier and he enjoys it. The contrast between Sergei's earlier life and now is staggering. We have to be honest in our dealings and that is just the way Sergei is. He understands more truths now and will not take the easy way out and commit suicide. Sergei's knows God's will is the most important thing to him and he remembers that the Bible says, "The first will be last and the last first."

Learning to understand God's will and how to be ready to follow it should be the primary focus of our lives. In Mathew chapters 6 and 7, it speaks about this kind of living. To stay in bed was not God's will for Sergei. We should not complain, and yet we do. We complain about life and do not even notice it. St. John said we should love each other and not judge but we still do it. We complain but should love and not complain. God said not to judge others but we judge each other anyways.

Zenaida Arsentevna

It was a lovely, sunny Thursday morning and snow was everywhere. Demetri and I rode in a taxi van to Zenaida Arsentevna's house. The blowing winds were both strong and vicious. We walked to an old wooden structure near a factory and the railroad. Zenaida met us at the door and welcomed us in. She knew we were coming, but she was still in her work clothes. This is still very common for Russian people. She excused herself, went into the kitchen and changed into a lovely blue dress. As she sat across the table from us, she began to tell us her story.

I noticed her father was very creative and always made the best of every situation. He planned well and raised his houseful of girls to work hard. The loss of all of ones possessions was very common when the collective farm started in the 1930's. You will notice how the people seem to accept their destiny and go on with life with very little complaining.

Another surprise for me was the way the family was treated as its husband and father was arrested. The words, 'enemy of the people' carried a substantial weight with it. Many of my friends tell me the people were afraid they would be next if they did not also oppose the arrested people and their families. Even some, church people were silent in supporting the family of the arrested ones.

Zenaida's mother was 56 years old when she gave birth to child number 10. This child was Zenaida and she was born in the Omsk Region, west of Novosibirsk. Two of the children in her family died earlier when they lived on a collective farm. In her village, Zenaida's father was the only educated person. He received his education in the Orthodox Church school and was smart. This is why the village people elected him as the village counselor. In Zenaida's family, there were only girls. Two of her sisters were married which left six still at home. The family owned their plot of land and it was divided up into smaller plots.

When her grandparents came from the Ukraine, the village lawyer said everyone could have a piece of land to build upon and farm. Zenaida's house was built at the edge of the village, but there were not enough people to work the land. Therefore, her father taught her oldest sister how to plow with the horse. He told his daughter the horse was gentle and she need not be afraid of it.

During these difficult times, many people wanted to join the collective farm. They believed this was the way to have a better life, but no one would lead this effort. The village people chose Zenaida's father to unite the people in this effort. He never used bad language in dealing with people, and at every celebration, he was the leader who put things in order. Therefore, everyone respected him.

Her family entered into the collective farm with two horses, two cows, chickens, pigs and the only threshing machine in the village. Upon the family's arrival, all of his animals and the threshing machine were taken. It was a common practice for the collective farm to take its members' personal possessions, use them frequently and often never return the items.

As the village farms united to join the collective farm, Zenaida's father traveled two and one half miles to complete the official paperwork. This caused him to be away from his own farm. He decided to ask the district's administration to give him a man to help his harvests. You will recall he had only daughters and naturally needed help. He wanted everything to be completely official and in proper order when the man came. When families were approved by the administration for extra workers, they moved to the edge of the village and received good land. If the administration rejected a family's request for extra help, they were given poor land. When good workers who were strong, had problems, they were required to move to the poor land. This is what happened to Zenaida's family. Some families worked hard and had good harvests while other families were weak and grew jealous of those with the good harvests.

At this point Zenaida wanted to speak more directly about her father. The family's neighbors were jealous and wanted to send her father to exile. Kostia, one of the respected men in the village, created false papers. Several men came and took most of her family away. Zenaida's grandfather did not go. He remained in the village to care for his son who had a back injury. Her father told his 15-year-old daughter to go stay with her uncle in another village, which she did.

The poor peasants learned Zenaida's family was leaving and came in and took everything out of their house. They took the furniture, a bench and everything else they could remove. One person was even embarrassed to see that in a trunk all the family had was a German made Singer sewing machine.

Kostia, and some other men, took the family to a new village. The family had suspected they would be taken to exile so they had prepared food ahead of time. Kostia did not. Zenaida's father invited Kostia to eat with him and he was very reluctant to do so.

Their travels continued by barge along the Opt River to their new home to the north and east, just beyond the swamp. On the way to their new location, some people fell off the barge and drowned because the waters were rough. When they arrived, there were many mosquitoes and the place was very, very uncomfortable. At first, they slept in hammocks. This was not comfortable, so Zenaida's father suggested they build barracks using veneer and blankets. The creation of walls allowed each family to have its own quarters. While in this new village, some of the children got sick because they had no milk. Once the families did have milk, they rationed it out in spoonfuls. Most of the children died because of little food, disease and no medical care.

In this new village called Kissalov, Zenaida and her family met some Germans who did things in a very quality way. Zenaida said, "Papa got attached to them and he was chosen to be the leader of the exile village because he was educated." Zenaida was now three years old. A woman cared for she and her sisters, but beat them for minor infractions. The children were afraid of the woman and the older children were required to dig up roots for food or prepare the garden. As Zenaida grew up, she developed problems. At the age of three, she could not talk and her legs were crooked. The childcare worker said her problems occurred because her mother put a black blanket over her.

At this point, Zenaida's father had built a *banya*, or a small bathhouse like a sauna. Everyone took baths and washed their clothes in it. Later on, they moved into a barrack, or hut, which had one window and a door. The children gathered coal for their home at a nearby coalmine. Her father later got a job in the coalmine. Life in the mine was very difficult and every day men were killed in serious accidents. Zenaida's father thought about the unsafe conditions and his children. These thoughts prompted him to take a safer job as a fire stoker. One day he heard a man in the mine whistling a tune that went like this, "Oh I am just a poor sinner, but I am a believer. Yes, I am." Zenaida's father asked the man where the people went for worship. It was at this place of worship he became a believer.

In 1937, Zenaida's family experienced more difficulties. She was now seven years old. During the early morning hours, a black van arrived in their village. This van carried people known as the *Black Raven*. Their responsibility was to take people away to exile. Some people were afraid and left the village. For Zenaida's family, the *Black Raven* came and took them to exile.

The day her father was arrested, they were at the table eating soup. The man who came to arrest him felt sorry for him. This man said he would leave, but Zenaida's father must come to the commandant's office after supper. Many times her father said he was innocent and the whole family began crying. He told his wife he would return soon because he was sure he was innocent. Some of the people were told to report to the commandant's office ran away into hiding. Zenaida's father would not. After supper, he went to the office and the next day he was sent to the southeastern part of Russia. He loved his wife, children and their land very much. On several occasions, Zenaida said her father was a perfect man, meaning he was very mature and kind in every way. He never shouted at his family and had a very optimistic outlook. He was a good carpenter and had very good tools. Before he left, he instructed his children to care for his tools while he was gone. Of course, he hoped he would one day join his family again.

On the day after Zenaida's father reported to the commandant's office, his family was called the 'enemy of the people.' This meant their father was also an 'enemy of the people.' They also learned their daughter who was told to live with her uncle at age 15 was found by authorities and sent to exile.

As Zenaida's sister rode a train to exile, she met a woman who told her to give her all of her money. This woman combined her money with the girl's and went to see the train attendant. She asked the attendant to take the money and give her a paper stating the girl was under age. The paper this woman obtained saved Zenaida's sister her from being exiled, and ultimately allowed her to return to her family.

During this great time of turmoil, Zenaida's family was demoted in society, asked to move out of their house and forced to live in a 3-sided cabin. In this very small cabin, the walls were wet which created health problems. Her mother now had to work on the collective farm causing her health to quickly deteriorate. The chairman of the farm felt sorry for her and gave her an easier job. During the summer months, she guarded the fields of sunflower and poppy. In the winter, she did different jobs, including watching the slaughtering of sheep. She took some of the sheep fat and processed it. People also gave her liver from the animals. With this, she made pies for the children. Each child was allowed only one pie. When Zenaida's mother could not work, the children did her work for her.

One day, a collective farm boss came by and asked what they had in their pockets. The family showed him and he saw they were very honest people. Some people who lived on the collective farm stole grain from the combine, but Zenaida's family did not steal. She was good at tying up the sacks of wheat and that is why they had bread. She was also able to take some wheat home because of her hard work. The people always strived to work hard because they were afraid. They were given a certain number of days to work and told if they did not work, they would go before the court and face trial.

When Zenaida's worked on the collective farm, she completed different jobs when there was snow on the fields. During the summer, she helped mow hay, lead bulls from one place to another for breeding and worked on the combine. She can still do that today. She also became very good at tying up the sacks of grain as the combine rolled along. Zenaida worked on the collective farm until 1947. Before she left, people teased her and called her and her family *kulaks*. *Kulaks* were the wealthier farmers and business people of earlier years.

Zenaida left the collective farm and began studying in a railway college. She paid for college with a scholarship she received. This scholarship allowed her to live in the dorm, eat bread and have a free ticket to travel home at her choosing. While in college, her friend discovered House of Prayer the name of all Baptist churches in Russia. She and Zenaida were invited to visit the church. They saw a large number of people and there were no problems. The Russian government did not like the young people attending church. It pressured the youth so much when a girl tried to get a job. However, she was not denied because she went to church. Zenaida knew this and yet she was not afraid to let others know she was a believer.

After college, she was sent to Kemerovo where she got a job. Zenaida's boss did not oppose her faith, but the boys she worked with did laugh at her. One day, a man from her church came into her place of work. Zenaida and this man began dating and were later married.

STORIES FROM TOMSK:

A City 4 Hours North of Novosibirsk

Isver Feodorovna and her Family

Feuder, Isver's father had two wives. His first wife died of pneumonia and left him to raise three children. While living in Novosibirsk, he met and married his second wife, Maria. When they met, she was already a believer and a member of the Baptist church. Maria's first husband died. She was left to raise one child. Together, Feuder and Maria were raising four children. From their union came two more children, Isver and a child after her.

Isver remembers October 25, 1937, very clearly. She was five years old and it was the last time she saw her father. Located in their family's library was a large, old Bible about 2 feet by 3 feet square with big, gold pictures inside it. That day, her father took out the Bible, put Isver on his lap, and the NKVD (*Black Raven*) came in and arrested him.

He told the men he wanted to pray with his family before they took him away. The NKVD (*Black Raven*) said, "OK, we will come back in two hours and if you denounce God, we will leave you at home, but if not, we will take you away." Feuder's wife said, "Run away." But he said, "If I do, they will come back and get you." When the NKVD (*Black Raven*) came back, Feuder told them he would never denounce his God, and so they arrested him. Isver's mother tried to follow Feuder, but one of the arresting men closed the door and would not let her out. Isver cried very, very much for her father.

The fearful *Black Raven* had struck again. Isver and her mother wanted to know where they took him. Because they could not get this information, went to a prison and waited. There were many people at the prison trying to get information about their loved ones. Finally, one person came out and said, "Why are you waiting. The men have already been shot."

Isver and her mother returned to the prison and received a document stating Feuder was shot and killed on October 28. He was a man who never compromised. He did not allow cigarettes in his home. If a man smoked and wanted to come into his home, he would say, "This is God's house. It is holy." He did not compromise his beliefs in the prison and as a result, he was killed.

Isver's father liked to joke. He was also very generous. Her mother and father regularly gave money to the church for the building and other needs. They sold their jewelry, including their wedding rings and gave the money to the building fund. Some people asked where did they get the money. Feuder would smile and say, "There is a tree outside with things of gold under it, and I took it from there."

The following years were very difficult. Maria could not get a job when Feuder was labeled as an 'enemy of the people.' After his arrest, it was even more difficult. Life for the family was very hard. They needed money for food, so Maria sowed clothes. With this money, they were able to purchase a cow, which was wonderful. This enabled the family to sell milk and purchase bread.

After Isver was grown, she worked in the Lenenski Region in Novosibirsk. While here, she was able to look at some documents pertaining to her father's death. Her healing process had begun. During her search, she found one document stating her father had died from pneumonia. A second document revealed he was killed. In this second document, it said he was an 'enemy of the people.' Either way, it was tragic how she lost her father at such a young age.

As Isver remembered her father, she also remembered her mother. Her mother Maria, was an active member of her church. When she was 17 or 18 years of age, she attended conferences in Novosibirsk. This was not difficult for her because she lived there. She sang in the choir and participated in other activities. During the war, she preached because there were no men. This was very common during these years. Maria, and two other believing women, led the church.

By 1923, Maria had been involved in the Baptist church for 70 years. At 90 years of age, Andrei Karlovich who was pastor of the church in Tomsk at that time, visited Maria and she asked him to not remove her from Group 10. This group was composed of the main leaders of the church who did the planning and organizing of all the meetings. By this time, she was very old and it was hard for her to go to church, so Maria became a very strong prayer warrior. As one of the ten chosen leaders in the church, she wanted to continue to offer strong leadership to the church through prayer.

I enjoyed the time I spent interviewing Isver. She was about 80 years old, and full of life and joy. It was at the pastor's home in Tomsk where she graciously met with me to discuss her father and family. As she told her story, she continually smiled and laughed. After all of the suffering she had gone through, she still had such a joyful, sweet spirit. It was a great challenge to me in my Christian life. The tears she shed for her father, as she saw him taken from the family, created much suffering for her. Yet, her father's absence had not in any way dampened her joyful spirit. Obviously, God's grace was abundantly sufficient.

As she was leaving, she asked if the women in our churches in America wore pants to church. I said, "Yes." She then told me how she disapproved of this practice. I smiled and said very little because Phyllis and I experienced this briefly during the nine years we worked with our Baptists friends. Her opinion did not in any way take away from the profundity of her story. She is still my hero.

Pavel Alekseevich

Pavel Alekseevich was the second cousin of Sergei Vecillovich, my wonderful host in Tomsk. Sergei is a retired pathologist and remains pastor emeritus of the main Baptist church. This family of believers lived in the city of Cherkessk, which is located in Stavropolsky Krai. It is found in the extreme southwest part of Russia bordering on Georgia. Pavel was about 40 years of age and had five children.

In 1941, the war began. Pavel did not want to change his position about going to war. As a result, he was arrested and killed. Death in these days occurred in a large and deep pit filled with water and lime. Lime is a harmless chemical when it is dry. However, when it is wet, it boils with an extreme alkaline fervor. The smell and chemical reaction can be compared to very strong sulfuric acid.

As Pavel prepared to die, he and other men were lined up along the edge of the lime pit. Soldiers stood by those being executed. Upon command, they were pushed to their death. Fortunately, the individuals died within minutes. As their bodies slowly sank, the deadly and horrible chemical ate their clothes, skin, flesh and even their bones. Sergei remembers the screams as being "beyond description."

Sergei also recalled the story of a young underground group operating in western Russia, near the Ukraine. The group consisted of about 20 young people between the ages of 17-24. It formed a resistance group against the German soldiers, also known as the Fascists. They used a code system to send messages to one another and thought they were being very careful as they explored different ways to oppose the Fascists.

World War II continued. So did the group. Its bravery increased and its members employed different ways to wreak havoc upon the Fascists. Ultimately, the group was discovered and the Germans threw them into the lime and water pit, just like Sergei's cousin, Pavel. Their deaths were just as horrific as Pavel's.

Abram Abramovich

Abram Abramovich was a preacher who lived in the Altai Region, which is south of Novosibirsk. One day the government came, took his farm animals, house and furniture for the collective farm, and sent he and his family to exile in Tomsk, north of Novosibirsk in central Russia. The county is very large and covers 198,125 square miles. Once he and his family were in Tomsk City, they were put on a barge and sent down river to a small town called Cardasok located in the northern part of the Tomsk Oblast. Within this area was a very thick forest known as Taiga. The Taiga was a horrible wilderness full of wild animals and swamps. The winters were cold and freezing. The summers were wet, full of mosquitoes and numerous wild animals made it impossible to escape. Gnats were also a horrible menace to the eyes, nose and mouth as those in exile worked.

It was here that Abram continued his preaching. He also taught a Sunday school class. Other families were sent to Taiga. Life here was very difficult and many people died. There was virtually no food. Abram's two youngest daughters died from starvation. His wife, Ustenia Petrovna, was very strict with the family's food and divided it out into very small portions. As his family sat around the table, they all hoped they would eat. At the end of a meal, they would leave with tears in their eyes because they were still hungry. Children only played games about food. When they slept, they dreamed of food. In the end, many people died because they could not properly divide their food out over a long period.

In 1937, Abram was arrested for three reasons and taken away. He was sent to the far northeastern part of Russia near Alaska. This place was a bay, called Boka Ola and it was near the Bering Straight. He spent 10 years here in exile. Why? The first reason for his arrest was that the NKVD (*Black Raven*) saw his preaching as an act that did not favor the collective farm concept. Reason number two was because he said there was no gold in Taiga. The NKVD (*Black Raven*) had told the people of Taiga, "You have gold; look for it." They looked under every potato and did not find any. Abram knew this. After he was arrested, one of the NKVD (*Black Raven*) told his wife, "We know you have no gold, but because he said there is no gold, we must send him to exile for 10 years. We must carry out our orders."

The final reason was he would not allow his son to paint a picture of a believer in school. Abram's children went to school and his son Peter became a good painter. One day he was asked by the teacher to paint a picture of one of the boys who was a believer. Abram would not allow Peter to do this. The teacher denounced Peter and this contributed to Abram's arrest. Peter was 14 years old at the time this happened.

While in exile, he was a good worker and made barrels. This allowed him to send some money to his family. One time he was able to include some money with a letter to his family. He was also a good cook and enjoyed writing letters to his family. After some time, the correspondence with his family was cut off. This is when the family felt his life was taken.

Between 1940 and 1941, Abram's wife, Ustenia died. Peter, Abram's son was now 20 years old. He was working as a fisherman, but could not eat the fish. His sisters worked taking branches from trees to make medicine.

In 1944, Peter was taken into the working army because he was German. He was sent to a small town called Komsomolsk-na-Amure near VladiVostok. He worked in a large building that provided support to the Red Army. He then was sent to Tomsk where he assisted the commandant in observation work and later was a pensioner. He became a believer between 1947 and 1948. In 1966, he became a preacher.

In 1953, rehabilitation [the government began to restore the names and health of those who had been in prison] began in Abram's family, and after many years, they received a report stating Abram died from a heart attack. Perhaps this was the truth; or maybe not. People said that during Abram's judgment from the government, his face was shining like an angel. Abram believed he would be killed in Boka Ola. It turned out he was right, but his death in exile was a blessing for his family. How you ask? It became a blessing in a way that sorrow, pain, and difficulties brought the family closer together. Through this tragic event in their lives, every member of the family came to know God personally. Abram's belief became an example of being faithful to God.

Roman Nikolaievitch

Pastor Sergei Vecillovich and I arrived at the apartment of Roman Nikolaievitch in Tomsk. The building was not well maintained. Roman appeared elderly, sick, extremely thin, in need of a good shave and even some good food. He also had difficulty speaking. It was obvious this dear Christian man had not been well cared for.

We discovered both his wife and son were alcoholics. They lived with him and were the primary occupants of this very dirty, roach-ridden, very unkempt apartment. The tragedy was, four wonderful children lived here too and they needed much care.

After our arrival, we were offered a small glass of mineral water with lemon. Sergei declined but I felt compelled to trust God and take it. The Lord was gracious to me; I did fine. We began talking with Roman about his life. Pastor Sergei tried to get him to remember how his father had suffered during the communist era. Roman tried, but could not think very well. He seemed to try but the words would not come.

While talking with Roman, his wife expressed interest in hearing English from an American. She was intrigued with our presence. Pastor Sergei was a very effective witness to both Roman and his wife. Only the Lord can deliver them from the terrible addiction that has been controlling their lives for years.

My heart certainly went out to Roman who was being neglected in his later years. He certainly deserved much better care than he was getting; however, when individuals let alcohol dictate their decisions, no one can do much about the situation.

Vera Vladimirovna

It was a lovely day in May 2005 when Pastor Sergei, his wife Gala and I walked from their flat to Vera Vladimirovna's flat in Tomsk. The flowers along the street were just beginning to peak their heads up through the cold Siberian soil. The winter snows had melted. Some of the soil was still frozen, but it gave life to those beautiful flowers. The flowers were unusually beautiful because the soil had a gray and unpleasant look to it as if it had not been tilled and reinvigorated.

Vera welcomed us in and began telling us her story while her invalid husband sat nearby. At the time of our interview, she was 90 years old. She had beautiful clear blue eyes that were full of life. Vera had a cough that day, but she still was very willing to share her story with us. Her husband suffered a stroke and could not function too well. She still attended church when she could. Throughout the interview, I clearly saw she had not let the problems of life keep her from fulfilling her purpose.

Vera spent some of her younger life lived in Lublatee in Novgorod County. This is near Krasnoyarsk, between Novosibirsk and the east coast of Russia. Her village burned during WWI, but the Latvians came and rebuilt it. This pleased the Tsar very much. Germans also came to the village which made it cultural.

Each of the personal farm steeds in Lublatee contained a beautiful garden with different kinds of fruit trees. Vera's home also had many beautiful flowers in her garden. She said, "It was God's creation." After seeing the outside of her home, Vera took us inside and showed us some very old photos. We saw pictures of her home and garden. Another picture was of Uncle Yulee Karlovich Kalminch, his wife and their children. Vera and Yulee's families held celebrations together twice a year, at Christmas and in the summer. Vera also showed us a picture of a whole village of believers and non-believers.

Vera began her story by telling us about Uncle Yulee. He was from Latvia and was one of the first people to begin living in the village in Lublatee. Before moving to the village, he completed his teaching degree at the university. Yulee then moved to the village and organized a school. He also started a church and became its pastor. Everyone who came to the village listened to what was said about both the school and church. Young people from the Russian villages nearby also came on Sunday's and listened to the choir. The little church had an excellent choir. They sang songs in both Latvian and Russian so the Russian young people could understand. This was considered entertainment for the youth during these times since there were no cinemas. Everyone seemed to enjoy the singing of the Christian songs. Yulee also noticed non-believers attended the church because it was a place to meet. The village became a wonderful place to live. No one drank, smoked, stole or used bad language. Everyone was free to go anywhere in the village and not see or hear these negative things. Everything was clean and orderly until 1931.

On April 5, 1931, both the Orthodox and Baptist churches observed the Easter holiday. It was that day the NKVD (*Black Raven*) arrested Yulee and all of the Baptists in Lublatee. They were sent to Hakasia located in Krasnoyarsk Krai, a region about 1,000 miles east of Novosibirsk. The communists sent these people to exile because they were not living by their laws. Communist law stated children under 18 could not go to church. It also said that if a church existed, the government would choose the pastor. Yulee's church chose to live by its own laws, which were God's laws. After that day, the church remained but worship was no longer allowed. The communists came and took over the building. They used it for a Red Club and said, "There is no God." The church members replied by asking, "What kind of church is this if there is no God?"

Sometime in 1932, the communists decided to till the land in front of the church building. The tiller came with two horses. They prepared the land for planting but a tornado came. It threw everything very high up in the air, including the horses, plow and the tiller. When it all came down, the man and horses were dead, the plow was destroyed and the church building was gone. The tornado had lifted the church up off its foundation and took it completely away!!! To this day, no one knows where it went. Some people smiled and said the church could have landed in a forest. Therefore, people searched the forest, but did not find it. The church had completely disappeared. At this point in the story, Vera showed us a picture of the church before the tornado.

Vera's house was located in front of the church and the road from Leningrad to Novograd came through her land. As she grew up, she listened to people describe the history of her land. On her land, located near the road, were three asp trees. These trees were called German Asp because one side was white and the other was green. When people traveled this road, they knew where she and her family lived because of these trees. Travelers also knew about their church. Yulee's church was unique because baptisms took place inside the church since there were no rivers or lakes nearby.

For many years after the tornado, people from Latvia and other locations came to Lublatee. They would see what was left of the church's foundation and where baptisms took place. The communists observed these events and smiled with a bad smile. The destruction of the church building meant they could no longer carryout their activities in Red Club. Ultimately, the communists saw there was a God and later forbid any churches in the village.

Yulee and his family lived in exile in Hakasia until 1935. This is when they were sent to Berlukski, located by the Chulin River in Krasnoyarsk Krai. Vera was now 20 years old. Her Uncle Yulee did not want to leave his extended family in Hakasia. Therefore, everyone in Vera's family agreed to go with him. He asked the commandant in Hakasia if the whole family could move with him. His request was granted, but later on, he was sent alone to another place nearby. While in Hakasia, he did not preach. When Vera's father died, Yulee did not attend the funeral because he was afraid and did not want to preach.

While living in Chulin, she realized she wanted to go to school. She wrote a letter to Nickolai, Lenin's wife, for permission to study in school. Permission was given and she left to study. She began studying, but had trouble because her Russian was poor. Because of this, her marks were bad and the teachers only gave her passing grades. When it was necessary to write compositions, her teacher gave her good marks for content but said she had poor sentence construction. She was good in math and science, and enjoyed it very much. When she completed the seventh grade, the commandant stopped her and would not allow her to continue because she was now required to go to work.

In 1940, a document was released from Stalin stating that children under the age of 12 were not under the control of the commandant. Everyone else, however, was under his control, especially those with no documents. Vera was no longer under the control of the commandant because she had documents. She received her documents and decided to go to work in Dixon, a northerly island at the North Pole. She was now 23 years old and had to prepare documents again.

Vera had her documents prepared by an old man. As he reviewed her pervious documents, he saw that she had come from the control of the commandant. He told Vera, "Don't ever let anyone see this document because you will be stopped immediately. And don't tell that you were sent out under the commandant." The man also noticed her Latvian name was Misza, which was the name of a muscle man. This was not good when making documents.

She arrived in Dixon to find many people from different factories who were trying to get documents so they could work. After all of the men had been called, she went into the office. The clerk asked, "Why have you come, because you are a woman?" Vera told the clerk she had been called up for an interview. This is when he saw Vera's given name of Misza in the big, thick book sitting on the table. He questioned Vera and she said, "I don't know what you mean about whether I am a man or woman, but I am a woman!" His response was, "Go home." Later on, someone encouraged her to change her name to a Russian name and she agreed. That is when she chose the name Vera. When she visits her Latvian family and friends, they still call her Vera, even though they knew her real name. Vera's nephew lives in Latvia now. His children asked her one-day why her name is Vera? "Because I was Misza which my father gave me, but now I am Vera," she said. The given name of Misza saved her life. Later in life, Vera moved to Tomsk, married and had a family.

On May 9, 2006, at a celebration, Vera's company gave her many beautiful flowers celebrating 60 years of victory since WW II. The very large bouquet was from both Holland and Russia. She found herself hugging it every morning.

In 2006, I again walked with Gala to Vera's house for a photo session. While she slowly welcomed us in, I noticed her energy was lagging. Her husband had now passed away and she felt his loss deeply. During this session, Vera graciously let me take her picture, but chose to sit instead of stand due to her age. As we walked down the stairs, this dear 92 year old Christian woman found enough energy to lean out her door and say in Russian, "Prevet Amerika." This means "Hello" in America. I stopped on the stairs, turned to her and said. "Ob bee zattelnee" or "Without fail."

Gala escorted me back to the bus station, helped me buy a ticket and showed me where to wait for the bus. Once I was on the bus and headed for Novosibirsk, I continued thinking about this dear saint, Vera. I could not get her out of my mind and felt the church members in Tomsk should visit her more often to dispel her loneliness.

Some of my thoughts were, "Here is a dear saint of God who saw many people killed and dumped into ditches prepared by caterpillar tractors and covered over." She also saw many miracles as she saw God solve the numerous problems associated with her documents. An entire book should be written about the laws of Russia, how they change and how the common people have to struggle to keep their documents in order just so they can work and do what they need to do. This Latvian sister in Christ is unequivocally my hero!

STORIES FROM KOLPASHEVO IN TOMSK COUNTY

Alexandra Gregorivna

On May 15, 1946, Alexandra Gregorivna and Rosa Valentine met at a meeting in Kolpashevo. Initially, Alexandra was afraid of Rosa because her skirt was made from very rough cloth and her cloth boots were tied to her feet with rope. In addition, she had gray hair and wrinkles on her face. Even though Rosa was only 30 years old, she looked like an old woman already. As the women talked, Alexandra learned her nickname was Maluta; Rosa was the youngest of 16 children, and her father was a simple engineer who worked at the post office.

Alexandra also learned that before Maluta moved to Russia, she worked with logs that were floated from the north down the river by barge. The women used poles with hooks to retrieve the logs from the river. On occasion, the hooks slipped off the poles and the logs rolled back into the river. Many women were crushed and killed by the logs when this occurred. Maluta's work was difficult and it made her very bitter.

After Maluta's move to Kolpashevo, life became a little easier and she worked as a house pianist. At first, she was not paid; therefore, Alexandra and her family tried to help her as much as they could. In 1956, Maluta married a Russian man. Sometime after that, she worked at a musical house where she taught many students who felt she was a wonderful person that not only taught them music, but how to live.

By 1961, the KGB (*Black Raven*) started interrogating her on a monthly basis. Approximately one week before each interrogation, she worried about what would happen; and after it was over, she was very upset because of the degrading remarks made against her. The authorities tried to destroy her character and this made it even more difficult for her to live a moral life. Nevertheless, Maluta did not complain about her life. Instead, she was very thankful that she was alive. You see, Matuta now knew Jesus Christ as her personal Savior and this made all the difference. She never let the evil nature of men dictate her attitude toward life; she remained positive.

In 1972, Maluta discovered she had leukemia and decided to return to Riga, Latvia. Upon her return, she learned that the Nazis killed all of her brothers and sisters. On July 26, 1972, she died and was buried in Riga. In 1987, Alexandra visited the grave of her dear friend who had suffered so. Alexandra was very gracious to tell about her special friend. As you noticed, Alexandra told us very little about herself. That is because of the love she had for her friend. The title for this story should be *Maluta*, but I am thankful to Alexandra who told me this story.

Agapia Ivanovna in Kolpashevo

In 1930, the *Black Raven* came and arrested the father and brothers of Agapia Ivanovna; the rest of the family was sent to Siberia. Agapia was only four years old and was too young to understand what had happened. At the time of her father's arrest, there were nine people in the family, her parents, five children and her grandparents. Before her father's arrest, he served in the army for the Tsar. Because he had been an officer in this army, the *Black Raven* arrested him. Agapia's father was not the only person arrested at this time. Anyone who was associated with the Tsar was arrested and the Tsar was shot.

After ten years a man came to Agapia's house looking for her mother. He explained that he had served in the army with Agapia's father. Both men were in prison together and became well acquainted. They exchanged addresses so when one of the men was released, he would go to the other man's family and tell them what happened in prison. As this stranger talked to Agapia's mother about her husband, everyone began to cry and scream. One younger sister cried very loudly and the man tried to comfort her. When Agapia's mother heard about her husband, she still held out hope that he was alive. She even hoped that one day they would be reunited because she had heard this happened sometimes; he never returned. The man spent the night at Agapia's house. The next morning he went to find his own family.

Agapia's mother was a member of the Orthodox Church, and as a believer, she prayed a lot. In those days, there were very few Bibles; however, she knew her Bible very well and tried to tell the children Bible stories from memory. Even when the family was sent to Siberia, Agapia's mother told the family members they needed to pray. During this period, the family was very thankful that Agapia's mother taught them about God and Jesus Christ. They believed every word their mother said about how God existed. It made it easier to cope when they suffered oppression and had to move from one village to another.

After many moves, Agapia's family finally stayed in one village named, Novougono. It was here that her mother worked very hard and applied for a job scrubbing floors at the school. Because the school's director noticed she worked very hard, she asked him if her family could stay in the village. He agreed, and the family stayed there for two years. This was when they moved to another village.

Life for the family became very difficult again. Each person received about 200 grams of bread, or two thin slices, for the day. Throughout these challenges, Agapia finished the seventh grade year of school in this village; however, the family moved again before her eighth grade year. Before this move, Agapia's mother suggested she not return home, but instead apply for a job in this village. She did just that and worked for some time.

This was the time in Agapia's life when some woman from Tomsk invited young people to study at the technical college. She went to Tomsk, from the northern area of Tomsk County, and studied. After her arrival, one woman helped Agapia locate her uncle who lived there. As she walked along the streets, Agapia asked every police officer about the address of her uncle. Finally, she found him and asked if she could sleep there that night.

The next day, she enrolled in the technical college. Some staff members introduced me to one of the teachers who helped her choose radio techniques as the focus of her studies. After she studied this topic for two years, she was privileged to go to Novosibirsk, Azerbaijan or Sakhalin. Agapia wanted to stay close to her mother and family, so she agreed to go to work in Varnavin, located in the Tomsk district. She worked at the radio station from morning until evening and lived there too because there were no houses to live in. A second person should have worked with her, but he was too busy, so Agapia did the work for both. It was at this job that she met and married Evon Feudervich, a man who had just returned from serving in the Red Army. From Novosibirsk, the couple moved to Kolpashevo.

Sometime during their courtship, Agapia revealed she became a believer during her time in Tomsk in 1964. This was when Evon told her he wanted to get rid of her. In response, Agapia told him that the Bible said that if a man did not want to live with a Christian wife, he could give her a divorce. He said she should give him a divorce; however, he did not really want a divorce. On one occasion, Agapia attended the Baptist church. When she returned, her husband thought she had been to the Orthodox Church, which her mother and sister attended. Evon asked Agapia how the meeting was and she said it was ok. She also said, "I liked it very much." It was at that moment he wanted to hit her. Once she told him that she had attended the Baptist church, he wanted to hit her again.

This was when the couple started living a strange life. Evon wanted to beat Agapia because she was a believer, and often he asked for a divorce, but she also did not want a divorce. From that time on, she tried not to miss the meetings and attend church every Sunday. Every time Agapia went to church, Evon hit her; he tried to prove that he was the head of the family. One time he even pulled her hair and pushed her in all of the rooms of their apartment.

In 1989, there was a celebration of the Bible and it was during a time when Agapia was in Tomsk. While at this event, she told the organizer she would like to have a similar celebration in Kolpashevo. He told her they should prepare for it, so she went to the House of Culture to get permission. The person in charge of the House of Culture agreed; in the autumn of 1989, the community held their own celebration holiday. A number of brothers attended and a choir performed.

The church members in Kolpashevo were glad to have such an event and decided to find land and build a church. (Up until this point, the members had met in a house.) One woman said she knew of a house that was being sold at Drekela Street #20. In this house lived a Pentecostal woman who sometimes went to the Baptist church. The church members purchased that house, and prayed and asked God to send them a pastor. In 1996, Victor Kyutchukov became the pastor.

After this, Agapia went to Novosibirsk for an operation on her eyes, but it was too late to have her eyesight restored. She felt this was God's punishment because during the times when she acted as the representative of the state in Kolpashevo, she only talked about her life at home. She told the city leaders about what her husband did to her and they discussed it. Maybe because of this, the judge told her husband he could no longer hurt her. After that, Evon did not hit her anymore. They lived together until Evon died in 2003. Agapia is now blind, but she is still alive.

Throughout Agapia's life, she did not let her blindness, or failing vision, keep her from being enthusiastic. She kept a smile on her face during my entire visit. In addition, I could tell she loved her Lord, the Savior who had been faithful to her all of these years as she lived with a man who did not know God, or want to know God. Agapia is a precious saint of God!

Peter Evanovich

Dear reader, prepare your heart before you read this story!!

In 1931, Peter Evanovich's family lived in Omsk and was forced to leave their home, two horses, two cows and many other farm animals and go to Tomsk County, north of Novosibirsk County. During their departure, their house, their possessions and all of their farm animals were given to the collective farm that was run by the government. The *Black Raven* had struck again!

As the family rode the ferry to Kolpashevo, in Tomsk County, they experienced horrible events. When the passengers were sick or died, the soldiers put their bodies in a bag and threw them into the river. One day, four-year-old Vanya, was sick. Peter's mother prayed that he would die and not be put into the sack alive. He died; his body was placed in the sack and thrown into the river. On another occasion, Little Olga, the youngest of the three daughters, was sick. Peter's mother prayed the same prayer for her two-year-old girl. Eventually, Olga died and she too was placed in a sack and thrown into the river. God answered the prayers of this faith-filled mother and spared her the stress of knowing her children did not suffer fear while sinking into the water.

After Peter's family arrived in Kolpashevo, his father saw all the fish and animals and said he was glad he was oppressed and sent to this place; perhaps his family would survive. The family was given one shovel that they used to dig a place to live. By spring, all of the new residences of this community had built a barracks in which each family had its own small space. Eventually, Peter's family built their own house on land they were given. Peter's father also found work as a fisherman on a boat with other men, and at night, he worked in the office. Within that office was a Bible; Peter's father read it daily because he was a believer.

In 1937, the *Black Raven* came on horseback, arrested Peter's father and nine other men and took them to the local prison. Because the men were taken at night, no one knew their final destination. That year, a great denunciation of the people occurred. When a man rolled a cigarette with paper that had Stalin's picture on it, he was sent to prison. At another time, a woman within their village asked to live with Peter's father. Because he was a married believer and refused, the woman became very angry. She went to the authorities, told them he was a believer and that he had a Bible that he read. As a result, the NKVD (*Black Raven*) arrested Peter's father and took him away; he never returned. Peter believes his father was shot sometime during the 1950's and buried in the large ditch beside the Opt River, on the western side of Kolpashevo. (A plaque is now posted by the riverbank memorializing the people killed and buried in that ditch.)

The ditch was a large, rectangular hole that contained the bodies of 1,000 people who had been shot. The *Black Raven* had not only been responsible for the arrests of these individuals, but also for their deaths. Unfortunately, each person, which included Peter's father, had been arrested under false pretenses and was innocent of any crime; however, they still died a horrific death.

As the years passed, the ice continued to flow north. As it did, it removed some of the dirt from the end of the hole. One morning during the late 1980's, as a man conducted some business near the river, he looked up and saw a body floating in the river; he called the police. The KGB came, removed this body, and tried to sink it to the bottom of the river. One woman from the village witnessed this event and cried out, "That is my husband." She noticed he still had red, natural colored lips because the permafrost had preserved his body. Peter's neighbor also saw a body floating, so he told the police. The police said, "Don't worry; these bodies are from the great hole." The dead bodies appeared clothed and the faces had expressions, even though all of the bodies had a hole in the back of the head. Peter thought it strange that the way the bodies appeared made the people look like they were still alive.

The authorities determined they needed a way to permanently get rid of the bodies, so they cut some up and tried to sink them to the bottom of the river.

The villagers began to watch this operation, so the KGB (*Black Raven*) cordoned off the area so no one could see what they were doing. It took the police one week, while working both day and night, to accomplish this task. Despite their efforts, there were frozen bodies that would not sink. Therefore, they put wire around the body parts and tied something heavy to them.

Life was very difficult for Peter's family, and they were afraid they would not survive. It was when Peter's mother was asked to become the head of the port in the storeroom that things began improving a little bit. Her responsibilities include writing some documents that released products for the ships. Because of this job, Peter's family was given some products that saved them. While his mother worked, Peter completed his schooling through the fourth grade. He was then told that if he wanted to continue his studies, he had to go to another place, so he did. He finished the fifth grade; however, when he started the sixth grade, the authorities called him and informed him he was the son of an 'enemy of the people.' This meant Peter could go into exile in some other place in Siberia and would live there until he died. Peter spent 14 years in exile and was then released.

By 1954, Peter was out of exile and was rehabilitated; however, he could not go anywhere because he had no documents. He was accepted into the army for three years and when he returned, his sister had gotten a job where she received a half bag of rye bread for her labor. It was now 1958 and that was her first salary. By

1962, Peter had moved back to Kolpashevo where his mother and sister still lived. From here, he moved to Irkutia, located in northeastern Siberia, because the town needed a specialist. He lived and worked there for five years. Then, he was asked to move to the northern part of the country; he worked there two years. Finally, he returned to Kolpashevo.

In 1972, Peter moved again. This time it was to Tyumen, which is between Novosibirsk and Moscow, but further north near Surgut. He lived there until 1980 when he moved back to Kolpashevo and found people meeting in a small house. These people talked about God and Peter knew God was present at these meetings. He also knew God had always blessed him because his mother always prayed for him. Peter's mother passed away in 1994.

When Peter was middle aged, he did not think much about the arrest of his father and all that happened to his family. Times are different now because he thinks about what happened quite often. Peter started working at the age of eight; however, his document said he only worked for 30 years. This false information resulted in a very small pension. During 1992, a new law was created. It stated that any survivor whose relative had been shot could requisition the government and receive some money. This money was given as a payment for the stress the family endured because of the loss of their relative. Unfortunately, it was not until March of 2006 that Peter learned of this law.

Peter and his sisters still talk about those times and ask each other, how was it possible they survived? They now know it was because Peter's mother was a very strong believer who leaned completely upon God's protection and provision. Interestingly enough, all the members of the family lived long lives. Peter's grandfather served in the army for 20 years, returned home at the age of 50 and had three sons. He raised them, and those who were not shot, also lived very long lives.

Galina in Kolpashevo

There were five children in Galina's family and she was four years old when her father was taken to the army. Nine days later, her mother gave birth to the sixth child. Her father returned home to take his clothes, and after one look at the baby, he asked his wife why she brought another child into the world knowing everyone would die of famine. Many times, Galina's family moved from one village to another within Kolpashevo. With her father away in the army, times were tough; there was only one coat and one pair of boots for all six children. Galina said her brother looked strange when he wore the boots and coat that were made for a girl.

To earn money for the family, Galina's mother worked at a brick factory making bricks. One day, when her brother was carrying a load of brick material on his back, he fell and broke his neck. Moreover, because there was very little medial care, he died. Everyday, while the other workers ate lunch, Galina's mother and the children continued working so they could receive a little money for food. Galina's job was to give the wet brick to her mother that she then put into the kiln.

At the age of two, one of her sisters died from eating bad food. The famine was very severe which made survival very difficult. Two of Galina's aunts bore a total of 18 children and 16 of them died. The two living children moved to Kolpashevo. One cousin moved in with Galina's family and was considered a family member. This cousin married at age of 20 and died giving birth to her first child. The child survived and Galina does not know where this person is today.

As time passed, Galina's family learned their father and other soldiers had been locked in a train car for a week without food. Once the men came to a potato field, they dug the potatoes and each man received seven. Many of the men died because they ate the raw potatoes. The family heard what had happened because a man from the army who was in that group came to the family and told them their father was probably one of the ones who died there in the potato field.

After Galina's family learned about their father, they moved to another village and lived in a big room with five other families. Each family had their own corner. It was while the family lived here that one woman told the authorities about Galina's aunt played cards. At her aunt's trial, she was asked about certain cards and what they were. Her aunt did not know because she did not play cards. The aunt was released. The family later learned the woman spied on people as an informer and was paid for her stories. At another time, this woman reported to the authorities about another woman and that woman was sent to prison. Upon that woman's release from prison, she said, "I will bite her nose if I see her again." One day the imprisoned woman saw the informer in a store; she bit her nose. The informer returned home to the big room. That was when Galina's mother told her she must leave or she might be killed. The informer left.

On another occasion, Galina's sister worked with a woman who said there was government salt on the bank of the river. The woman encouraged Galina's sister and other children to get the salt and sell it. The children were caught and Galina's sister and friend were sent to prison for five years. Of course, it was unfair, because there was a law that said children under 12 should not be sent to prison.

Stories of when men who were arrested and shot

Russian entry

Архипов Николай Федорович. 1878 г., родился в деревне Быстрово Орловской губернии, проживал в г. Томске, пекарь Томского военного госпиталя. Арестован в 1938 г. Расстрелян.

English translation
Arhepov Nickolai Feudorovich. He was born in 1878 in the village of Bistrova Orlovskoi Province . He lived in the city of Tomsk, and was a baker in the Tomskova military hospital. He was arrested in 1938 and was later shot.

Russian entry
Дробчик Николай Климентьевич, 1902 года рождения, г. Ярославль, проживал в г. Томске, электромонтер в психбольнице. Арестован в 1937 году. Расстрелян.

English translation
Drovchick Nickolai Klementevich. He was born in 1902 in the city of Yaroslavl. He lived in the city of Tomsk and worked as an electrician in a psychiatric hospital. He was arrested in 1937 and was later shot.

The names of two of the men listed above were taken from a book given to me by Peter Evanovich. The book contained many names of people who were arrested, put in prison or shot. A second book also contained similar information. If you total up the names from both books, it equals 53,000 people who died during the difficult years of communism.

STORIES FROM BOLOTNOYE:

A County in Northern Novosibirsk

Anna Antonovna

Anna Antonovna lived with her parents in a village near Bolotnoye; a town that now has about 15,000 people and is located 50 miles north of Novosibirsk. When the children were young, they were often neglected. Their father was in the army in World War II and there was very little food. The family was not allowed to move to another place because they were watched and worked like prisoners. The family, including the children, had to be careful what they said because people were being arrested for any negative word said against the Soviet power. The believers were assigned the most difficult jobs, such as sweeping the streets or caring for the garbage. These times were exceptionally challenging since the Antonovna family were the only Christians in the village.

During those days, the government required every family pay a tax in the form of material products. If a family owned a cow, they were required to give to the government 200 liters [slightly more that 200 quarts] of milk per month, and 40 kilograms [88 pounds] of meat. If their cow gave birth, the calf was given to pay the tax. Families could keep their sheep, but were required to give its wool as a tax. Ownership of a goat meant the government received one and one-half liters of milk per month. Each family could own no more than two cows. If a pig was slaughtered, the skin was given to the government and the family kept the pig. In addition, if a family had more than one pig, they were taken.

The government expected to receive their tax payments, even if it meant the families would not have enough food. Anna's family was able to stay alive because they had a little garden outside of their kitchen window. The family used the cabbage to make borsht soup. Beets, carrots and potatoes were also grown and used regularly in their diet.

In the school, there were four grades and the educational focus was how to write. The children walked to school regardless of the weather. They had to take very good care of their coats because there was no money to buy new ones. Their shoes had holes so they used cardboard to keep out the water and dirt. Rainy days meant the children had to change the cardboard in their shoes because the old became wet and useless. Russians were, and still are, known for wearing very good clothes. When there was no money to purchase new coats and shoes, they believed times were hard.

After the war, when their father returned home they moved to Bolotnoye. Life became a little better and the intense persecution decreased some; however, there were still many problems. One day, while Anna's children were still young, she was called to the police station. Someone had sent letters to the police declaring that she and her family went to church. The police asked why she took her children to the church. She reminded the officer he was free to take his children wherever he chose and she chose to take hers to the church. She also insisted that he did not have any love for his children by not taking them to church. Anna also told him he was indifferent to people and even animals. She was astounded at her own bravery.

Anna and her family lived 15 kilometers (10 miles) from the church. As they traveled to church, people made fun of the family. They also made crosses like the Orthodox people and called them "Baptists" in mockery. This happened on the buses and on the streets wherever they went. One day, Anna asked an officer, "Why do some of the ladies have bruises under their eyes? Husbands cause these bruises which is abnormal behavior." As she and the police officer looked at one another, he clearly said, "Get out of here!" As Anna spoke these harsh words, she realized that only a Russian woman could speak to a government official in this manner. In the earlier days of Stalin, she would have gone to prison for speaking out like she did. Government officials were not the only ones who harass Anna. Young boys called her *Bagamolka*, which means a woman in prayer. Even though people shouted at them, they had great joy in their hearts and were always praising God for the difficulties in their lives. They recalled the verse that reminded them it is a privilege to endure insults and abuse for the cause of Christ.

In February 2006, Anna's mother died after living with her for 20 years. Anna remembered when her father came home from the war, people made fun of him because his wife was a Christian. Her mother was very passionate about her faith in God and would walk 18 kilometers (11 miles) just to attend church. While Anna was growing up, her mother worked nights so she could attend church with her children on Sunday mornings. In those days, employees were not given time off work, especially to attend church. Anna's mother had a sister, who lived in Caucuses and later moved to Bolotnoye, who was also a believer. It was through this sister that her mother came to Christ. God blessed them, protected them and fed them by His mercy.

Anna's mother had three children. One daughter is now a believer, the other one is getting closer each day, and Anna rejoices in this. When her father was young, he was strong but did not see a need for God. After Anna's father got sick, he turned to God in the same way his wife did. Earlier Anna's father scolded her for going to the church. However, after he was sick, he wanted the believers to come to his house and include him in the fellowship. He prayed to receive God in the wintertime when baptisms were not held due to frozen lakes and rivers. Before he died, however, he was baptized. Baptism is very important to Russian believers. Unfortunately, Anna's husband was not baptized before he died and now she questions whether he is with God. She does agree, however, that God is the final or ultimate judge.

After Stalin died in March of 1953, the country's remaining leaders lessened the amount of persecution they were inflicting on believers. The result was Anna's family was no longer despised in public. Anna always tried to get people into the church. She knew that if they trusted Christ, their lives would be better because the fighting would stop and they would have a better lifestyle. Russian families fought because there was no love and they did not know the true God.

Once the Russian people were given their religious freedom, the believers were very, very thankful and reveled in expressing their commitment to a very faithful God. They felt free to sing and praise God outside. Radio stations taught the Christian rules of life. God blessed the believers with spiritual freedom, and in return, they praised God without opposition and did not ridicule the non-believers in the community. Anna continues to feel the Lord will come soon and she looks forward to it.

Maria Vacillovna

In 1947 Maria Vacillovna met her husband after he returned from fighting in WWII for five years. Just before the two met, he asked, "Who is that girl?" He wanted to know because Maria had a smaller stature and he thought she was 15 years old. She was actually 20. Soon after this meeting, he took Maria to his home to get married.

Some individuals opposed the marriage; even Maria was not too sure she should marry him. Her mother did not like him because he talked too much. People told Maria that when this man was a child, he broke windows, climbed over fences and messed up people's gardens. Even though all of this was true, Maria tried to defend him. She told her mom the war had made a man out of him and his past was his past. Maria even reminded herself she might end up an unmarried woman if she did not marry him now. Her mother wanted her to wait and reminded Maria that childhood values usually are carried with an individual into adulthood. Nevertheless, Maria married this man. (As Maria reflected upon this time in her life, she wished she had listened to her mother and not married this man.)

After they were married, they lived with her husband's parents. While living in their house, Maria's father-in-law suggested he build a house for his foolish son while he was still alive or his son might end up living in someone else's house. The truth was, the man Maria married was not a very good husband. He drank too much Vodka and spent a lot of time away from their home. As a result, Maria taught her children to work hard through helping in the garden and gathering berries. One daughter even cared for the family's shoes by cleaning and organizing them in neat rows.

The year was 1957 when Maria, her husband and their children moved 100 kilometers (62 miles) from the village to a town named Quobeshev, located in the Novosibirsk Region. The town had been around about 300 years and was started during the period when people were being sent to the Siberian frontier. It now was known as a merchant's town.

While Maria and her family lived in Quobeshev, her daughter was a great student. The family was very proud of her success. Her teacher also praised Maria's daughter during the school's parent/teacher meetings. This daughter ultimately became a teacher of math and science in Bolotnoye. She had a son and Maria encouraged her daughter to have more children. The daughter did not want to because she did not like her husband's behavior.

Maria's grandson completed only eight years in secondary school. Therefore, he went to work in a factory controlled by Moscow. The factory made combines and it needed skilled labor to make these machines. Maria told her grandson if he continued working in the factory, he would remain a helper and not become a professional worker. As a result, Maria encouraged him to go to Novosibirsk and study in a technical school. He enrolled in the Riverboat Worker's College to learn about work on the riverboats. He liked this college, enjoyed wearing the sailor's uniform even more.

During our interview, Maria also talked about her mother. She told me her mother had become a believer. Maria said her mother faced many challenges during this time because believers had to meet in a different location each time they gathered because of the police oppression. Maria's mother encouraged her to go to church, but the police forbade; so, Maria slipped in anyways. The mothers in these gatherings told their children not to bow down when they prayed because it was forbidden; however, they could sing. If the believers did bow their heads when they prayed, the police beat them with hoses. The police also told the mothers to send the children outside because it was hot. Nevertheless, Maria's mother did not do this. Instead, she reminded her children that when it was hot at school the teachers did not send the children outside.

The police were not the only people to harass Maria's mother. Her neighbors mocked her by calling her names. They also poured slop, empty bottles and dead cats into her garden. Once the snow melted, Maria's mother cleaned up her garden and crying as she did it. Later on, a former friend came over and scolded Maria's mother for going to church. Maria asked why this friend had come over and interfered in her mother's life. She believed it was her mother's affair and if she wanted to go to church by her own free will then she should be able to do just that. It was then that the woman asked if Maria herself would go to the church. Maria said, "Maybe I will go. It is a possibility."

Maria's unsaved aunts even posed a threat to their own sister, Maria's mother. These aunts lived in Novosibirsk and planned to go on holiday. They were forbidden because they had a Christian sister, Maria's mother, in

Bolotnoye. These aunts did not read the Bible and did not want anything to do with God. The aunts wanted to find out the truth about their sister so they traveled to Bolotnoye. When they arrived, they beat their sister with a big wooden soupspoon, tore her dress to rags and left her in an indescribable state. Maria defended her mother by saying she did not drink or carouse around like some women; neither did she get in the dirt like some drunks. She reminded her aunts that on their own free will they went to the cinema. Maria concluded by declaring, "Mother is an old person and has a need to go to church for Christian fellowship and strength." Maria's mother was joyful that Maria stood up for her to her sisters. She felt God had sent Maria to defend her.

Maria's granddaughter also became a believer; however, she too had to go to church secretly. Maria's daughter and son-in-law opposed their daughter going to church. Maria asked her granddaughter how she found out about the church. Her granddaughter said she saw a sign telling about a Bible being on sale at the church. It was a long distance from her house to the church. Moreover, since her parents opposed her going to church, she asked Maria to come and defend her. Maria talked with her daughter and asked, "Would you rather that your daughter go out drinking with friends and carouse around with other teenagers and the like?"

The daughter and son-in-law never did trust Christ but the granddaughter continued to go to church and became a strong follower of Christ.

I leave you with one thought. Philippians 3:8 (NAS) says, *"More than that, I count all things to be loss in view of the surpassing value of knowing Christ Jesus my Lord, for whom I have suffered the loss of all things, and count them but rubbish so that I may gain Christ."*

Other believers who lived in Bolotnoye, Siberia during these difficult times elevated Christ above possessions and circumstances just like Maria Vacillovna and Anna Antonovna. The loss of possessions did not keep believers from progressing in their love of Jesus Christ. It was quite the contrary; they loved Christ even more.

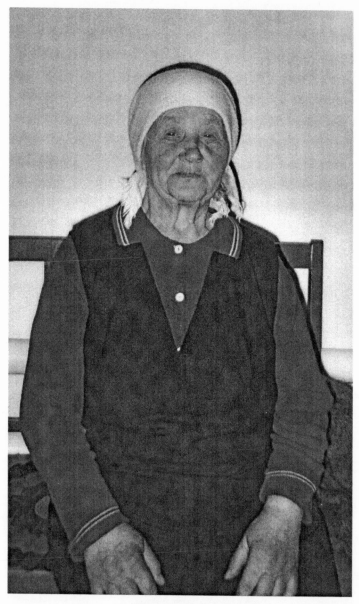

Maria in Bolotnoye

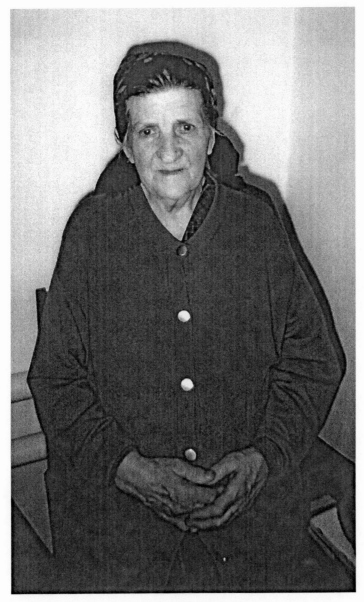

Anna

Alexei in Pestila

Alexandra

Agapia

Peter Evanovich

Galina

Vera

Claudia

Maria (Marussia)

Section II

STORIES FROM NOVOSIBIRSK

Yakov Zakarlovitch Komo

Komo Yakov Zakarlovitch was the grandfather of Ola Komova. Ola was also my tutor and secretary in the mid 1990's. She began our interview by talking about Yakov's time in the war. Yakov said that because the fighting on the front line was very intense, he prayed and asked God to save him. He told God that He saved his life, he promised to dedicate his life to serving God. God answered his prayer because when the battle of Leningrad was over, he looked around and found he was the only person alive.

He was released from the Red Army and went to the city of Keev which is the capitol of the Ukraine. As he walked along the road, he met a boy riding a horse. Yakov told the boy he was going to Keev to pray. The boy told Yakov he could pray here in the countryside and invited him to his home. Yakov wanted to continue his journey, but the boy's father encouraged him to stay and worship with the family because other believers were coming. As Yakov listened to the preaching, he told the worshippers he felt every word that was said was directed at him. He was greatly moved by the hearing of the gospel and found his heart was very thirsty for God's word.

He left those believers and made his way home to the Altai Region, several hours south of Novosibirsk. As Yakov's family, prayed before their meal, Yakov's wife noticed Yakov did not make the cross like other Orthodox believers. Therefore, she did not let him eat for several days. (This is important because it emphasizes that in Russia the wife runs the house.)

After Yakov returned home from the war, he purchased a Bible, and began reading it and studying it daily. He discovered people were not living according to God's word. Yakov also met some people who prayed a little each day and this encouraged him. Eventually, his Orthodox-believing wife repented and began developing a personal relationship with Jesus Christ. He and his wife were baptized in the Baptist church and became active members. Yakov then began preaching in the village and people began repenting and coming to faith in Christ. He learned the Baptist Union of Russia was in Saint Petersburg, the capitol of Russia at that time. Yakov went there and received his ordination as a preacher in the Baptist Union of Russia.

In October of 1917, a revolution began and the Bolsheviks began what would be years of persecution of all religious people. When Lenin, Stalin and several others took over the government, the communists continued their evil reign. Lenin died in 1924 of an aneurysm. This opened the doors for Joseph Stalin to begin his march toward gaining full control over the government. Within just four years, Stalin, which means steel, had all the power he needed to rule the country. The phrase, 'enemy of the people' became a key phrase used when arresting and persecuting people. Anyone who opposed the government was labeled an 'enemy of the people,' Va raog na roda in Russian.

During the beginning of Stalin's reign, Yakov and his family lived in the church building provided by the members in the village. He had a cow, horse, pig, chickens, ducks and several other farm animals. One day, the NKVD (*Black Raven*) came, forced Yakov and his family out of the church house and confiscated everything they owned. The family moved to Kazakhstan, and was fortunate to take some of their clothes with them. Life was difficult in this new location; however, Yakov continued to preach.

In 1927, the NKVD (*Black* Raven) arrested and imprisoned him for his faith. While in prison, the government did not allow him to have any communication with his family. The authorities said this was part of the punishment for being an 'enemy of the people.' In 1930, he was released from prison and he and his family moved back to Altai.

Persecution continued to take its toll on the Russian people. As a result, Yakov led 600 families to the wilderness of Siberia in 1931. The people traveled for 30 days and 427 miles to an area known as the *Taiga*, which today would be called a jungle. During the first year, the people chose a place that was not in a swampy area. They dug deep basements and cut down trees to build houses that were 90% underground. (Sometimes these trees fell in the wrong direction and killed people.) The community members also used only their hand tools to clear the land and plant their food gardens. The wilderness was beginning to be civilized and the people began making this place their home.

The members of this community were very strict with one another. So strict, that during the early years, if someone wanted to leave and return to an easier civilization, they were shot. After one year in the "*Taiga*," only 120 families were left alive; many had died due to starvation or the cold. This meant 480 families perished in this wilderness!

On April 6, 1937, Yakov was arrested and imprisoned again. This time the henchmen said, "Gather your things and come with us." These were the cold-blooded words commonly said by the *Black Raven*. Then three months later, his wife was taken from her children and put in prison too. She asked the henchmen what the charges were. They answered her with this question, "What American has been going to your home?" She was very surprised at their question because there was no American who had been at her home. Fortunately, three months later, she was released and allowed to return to her family.

Yet, one month after her release, the *Black Raven* arrested and imprisoned Yakov's brother. Six months after that, another brother was arrested and forced into prison. No communication was allowed between these prisoners and the family. After the WWII, the family asked the authorities about what happened to Yakov and their uncles. They were told Yakov died of an aneurysm and a brother died of a stomach problem. Neither story was true.

In 1987, Benjamin, one of Yakov's sons, and his sister asked the prison authorities in Tomsk what was the true fate of their father and uncles. At first, the government said the documents about their deaths were lost, but later the truth came out. Yakov and his brothers were shot with a rifle in 1937 as 'enemies of the people.'

Vladimir Stephanovich

Vladimir Stephanovich's grandfather moved from the Ukraine to Siberia in 1895. He lived in Zuravka, located in southern Novosibirsk County. At the age of twenty, Vladimir's grandfather and his brothers became soldiers in WWI. After serving in the army, he got married, worked hard and became the richest man in the village. He owned 20 cows, 11 horses, pigs, chickens, ducks and sheep. He also lived in a 4-room house and had many barns and sheds on his property. All of this was taken from him when he was sent to the collective farm at the age of forty.

While Vladimir's grandfather lived on the collective farm for those ten years, his brothers told him about an opportunity in a butter factory in southern Novosibirsk. The family moved and immediately started working in this factory. Vladimir's grandfather became a Malatillka . He became the only person in the village who received the wheat and removed the straw so it could be made into flour. It was hard work, but he had an electrical machine, an early form of the combine, that others did not have. It was through the work in this factory that the family made its money.

From 1928 to1930, some people arrived in their village and identified seven or eight people as *kulaks*. On February 17, 1930, the *Black* Raven arrested Vladimir's grandfather. Just one month later, on March 17, he was shot and killed. The authorities did not say they killed Vladimir's grandfather; they only said they sent him somewhere. After this, Vladimir's grandmother wrote letters to the government and asking that her husband be freed. In response, the government sent a sheet of paper with two points. The first said the purpose of the arrest was to kill Vladimir's grandfather. The second was to send the remainder of the family to exile in the northern part of Siberia.

The rest of the family was sent into exile to the northern part of Siberia. The members included the great-grandmother, grandmother, mother, three boys ages 15, 10 and 5 and a 6-month-old baby. During their trip to exile, the family first stopped in Tomsk. From there, they continued by boat down the Nurolka River. While traveling on this ferryboat, Vladimir's mother fell from the upper level and hurt her head. She was a strong believer and she knew God would help the family survive during their time in exile.

Once the family of Vladimir's grandfather arrived at the exile camp, they noticed it was swamp and woods. They quickly learned the purpose of exile was to kill people. The family also learned that the closest village was 70 kilometers (45 miles) away and many mosquitoes were present during the spring and summer months. As the family lived and worked in exile, they built a little hut for their home. Each month, the government gave every family member 50 grams of milk and 500 grams of flour. This was the only food the people in exile received, again, because the government hoped they would die.

As an adult, Vladimir's father also spent time in exile. He lived in an exile camp for two years in Krasnoyarsk, 1000 miles east of Novosibirsk. After he served his time, he was released and was allowed to rejoin his family. The government took him to Tomsk. If he wanted to see his family, he had to travel the remaining 300 kilometers (just under 200 miles). Therefore, he and two other men walked the remaining distance. Finally, after one more year, Vladimir's father was reunited with his family.

Vladimir's father lived in the village with his family for one year before Moscow issued a new law allowing him to move and look for a job. In 1933, he moved his family to the town of Prokorpis, located near Kuzbas in the Kemerovo Oblast, to look for a job. They lived in the town for one year before someone told him to write a paper of complaint to the government asking to be completely freed. (Vladimir's father no longer lived in exile; however, he still did not have any rights.) Vladimir said, "Scientists who made the nuclear bomb worked for free because they had no rights also." It was like being in prison again. He wrote the letter and after one more year, he received a document stating he was free.

It was now 1934. He was finally declared free and could pursue a job. He tried to get a job but could not because he had been a prisoner. For some reason, he lost these documents and had to get new ones. The new documents did not mention his former prison days. This made it much easier for him to find work.

The family moved to an area near Novosibirsk. While in this area, Vladimir's father noticed some people did not like them because they had been *kulaks*. As a result, the family found another place to live and moved to it. No matter where Vladimir's family lived, his father was very industrious when building some kind of housing or renting a house each time they moved.

As Vladimir shared about his family, he told me he did not learn much about his father until his father was 70 years old. Vladimir's father was always afraid that if he shared any information about his grandfather, he would be arrested again.

As we concluded the interview, Vladimir told me he served in Algiers for four years as a geologist. He read the Old Testament in French and children's books of the New Testament in English. He is now a professor in an institute in Novosibirsk and writes poems and prose.

He showed me one of his works in prose. He is a gifted writer. I felt quite inadequate in his presence.

Claudia Demetrivno

Claudia Demetrivno lived with her family in Novosibirsk during the difficult years of 1937 to 1945. In 1937, NKVD, (*Black Raven*), came and announced that her father, Demetri, was an 'enemy of the people' and would be taken to prison. Claudia's family members were Christians and worshipped God consistently. Because of their faith, a document was made that declared Demetri was an 'enemy of the people.' (Authorities often created false documents as a way to justify their guilt.)

One night, Demetri was taken away by the *Black Raven*. Claudia was 12 years old. She and her siblings cried as they saw their papa for the last time. Claudia's little brother, who was five years old, was asleep when their father was taken. Later, when the family asked him about his papa, he said some men came and took him away. He knew what had happened to his father, even though no one had told him.

When the *Black Raven* (NKVD) took Demetri, they also took the money that Claudia's mother used to purchase food. The loss of the money, and more importantly Demetri, was devastating to this family. Before Demetri was taken away, he was the only member of the family of six that worked. He earned a salary of 80 to 100 rubles per month and Claudia's mother spent 10 rubles per month on food. Her family was now left with no money for food.

One day Claudia came home from school and saw just a little bit of food sitting on the table. She ate it all because she thought her family had already eaten and had left this for her. When her siblings came in, they asked, "Why did you eat all the food?" What she ate was the food for the whole family and not just the leftovers. To this day, Claudia regrets what she did.

Claudia's family also looked forward to the summer and fall when they had vegetables from their garden, or *agarod*. The vegetables they grew saved their lives. The problem occurred during the winter months when the food ran out. On another occasion, Claudia's older brother went to the basement to get some potatoes; he discovered they were gone. Claudia's mother, who already worried where the next meal would come from, told the children not to be disheartened; other people were worse off. Her encouraging words kept their spirits up.

The family did find ways to meet their needs with very little money. Claudia's mother washed clothes for the neighbors so she could purchase food for the children. The oldest son enlisted in the army, which brought some financial relief for the family. In addition, the children gathered wood from outside to burn in the stove during the cold winter months.

One day while Claudia's mother was working, she learned from two other women that their husbands had also been shot. Claudia's mother wrote a letter asking about what happened to Demetri. After she received word about which prison he was in, she went to it and received a document. It said Demetri had been shot about two months after he arrived at the prison. The officials gave her some money that Demetri had earned while in prison, but not all of it.

Due to the family's financial situation, Claudia completed her schooling through only the eighth grade. She did, however, later attend nursing school which was free. Two brothers were also successful; one became a doctor and the other an artist.

In 2006, I received word that Claudia had passed away. She is now enjoying seeing her father again in a place where the only law is one of love and peace.

Allah Petrovno

Allah Petrovno's family lived in the Krasnoyarsk Krai Region, which by air is two hours east of Novosibirsk. She showed us pictures of her family while she told Olga and me about them and her life. She began by telling us about how both she and her husband felt the sting of the NKVD (*Black Raven*) because many of their family members were arrested and sent to prison.

Mesha was Allah's husband. His grandfather, Vacilli was a preacher who was taken to prison by the NKVD (*Black Raven*) during the purge of 1937. The purge was known as 1937, 38 when Stalin was arresting many people for virtually no reason at all. When the soldiers arrested Vacilli, he was working at the railway station. The authorities did not explain why he was being taken. They just took him and did not allow him to go home for his clothing or personal belongings. Once he was at the prison, three people judged him and told lies about him. They said he was a member of a Christian Evangelistic cult also known as a religious sect that wanted to overthrow the power of the government. The people also claimed the group wanted to kill Stalin. Because some people knew Vacilli would not return, they encouraged Mesha's grandmother to remarry because she was still quite young. She too knew her husband would not return, but declined to remarry because she loved him. Unfortunately, Vacilli was never heard from again.

Sometime between 1917 and 1918, Stalin's sadistic henchmen killed Allah's paternal grandfather by beating him with ropes in a village near the city of Krasnoyarsk. Therefore, this left Peter, Allah's father, without a dad at the age of 11. Peter had 10 siblings; however, five died before the age of two. Stephan, Maria, Peter and Andrei were taken to prison. Sadly, only Peter and Andrei returned after they served nine years of their 10-year sentence. Maria died in prison of starvation and Stephen was not heard from again. Since Peter's younger sister, Annya, was not arrested, she stayed with their mother until her death in 1949. She died in 1950 after she caught a cold while milking the cow in the cold weather.

The prison where Peter and Andrei served their sentence was located northeast of the Ural Mountains, several hundred miles east of Moscow, located in the Kirov Oblast. They worked in the forest removing trees. Sometimes the guards at the prison camp were afraid to give prisoners saws and axes; therefore, the men removed the trees with only ropes. Typically, a man climbed to almost the top of the tree and attached one rope to either side. Then, many men pulled on both ropes and rocked the tree back and forth until they pulled it down. Many men died in these prison camps due to the harsh labor, cold weather, poor food and virtually no healthcare.

As Peter was leaving the camp, he was told to sign a document stating he would not tell how he suffered while he was there. Upon returning home, Allah's mother and the children tried to get the facts from him; he would not tell them. Eventually, one story leaked out about the Vitamin C deficiencies that caused death for many prisoners because there was a lack of food. Prisoners did eat wild berries and an herb called Chitimsha. This herb was available in the early spring and provided vitamin C. The people said, "If you survive till spring when the herb comes out, you will live."

When Peter was released in 1946, the government did not give him any documents. (And to this day, if you live in Russia and do not have any documents that show who you are and what your qualifications are, you are considered a nobody.) Sometime after his release, a new law appeared which said anyone who had previously been an 'enemy of the people' could not live in big cities and must leave within 24 hours. Peter could travel in any direction he chose; however, he had to leave the city immediately.

Peter and his family were living in Krasnoyarsk, so they left and went to see his friend in Novosibirsk about a job. Because Novosibirsk was also a big city, he was forced to leave again within 24 hours. His friend told him about Isketim, a town about 80 miles east of Novosibirsk. It was the former prison camp, which was absolutely awful. In fact, in 2005, a documentary was created to show the terrible conditions people lived under in Isketim.

Within this town, Peter found a room, rented it and sent for his family. Once the rest of his family arrived, they rented half of a house because his wife and three daughters needed more space. The property owner was not very honest. Because some of Peter's things came up missing, Peter's wife encouraged the family to find better housing and they did. In fact, Peter bought some land and materials and built a very nice-sized house for the family.

While he lived in Krasnoyarsk, Peter graduated from the music school. This background enabled him to start a secular music school where he taught Beethoven, Bach and other great composers. Most of his students were from families that had been labeled 'enemies of the people.' In addition to teaching music, Peter had some other little businesses on the side that included working at a coal minor's club and in the chicken factory. He received what was considered very good pay, about 400 rubles per month.

The war was now over and a time of rehabilitation (help from the government to those who had been in prison) began for Peter and his family. He received a document from the government that stated that he was not proven guilty of any crime. There was one point where Peter could have been found guilty. After he was released from prison, he was given 900 rubles, 100 rubles for each year he worked while in prison. Peter's wife, and Allah's mother, wondered what to do with this money. She took the money and purchased a black fur coat for her three girls. All three wore this coat as they grew into it.

Allah concluded our interview by telling me this story. One day the authorities witnessed some men building a building. They decided to inflict suffering upon the builders. As a punishment, the authorities put one man up against a wall and built another wall two feet away from him. The wall was bricked up to the ceiling, trapping the man inside and causing him to starve to death. It was the authorities way of using another cruel method to kill a man. The idea of variety intrigued them.

Evon Vasilovich Pavlov

Evon Vasilovich Pavlov was born in 1896. When he was four years old, his father Vacilly moved the family from Lithuania to Omsk because they were believers and attended the Orthodox Church. Vacilly was an educated man, and after their move, he worked for the railway in Omsk. It was not hard to find a job because there were not many educated people around at that time.

Evon, married in 1920. His daughter, Luba, was born in 1921. His son, Vacilly, who was named after his grandfather, was born in 1923 and became a believer later in life. Four other children were born to Evon and his wife, Anna, between 1921 and 1937.

Because music played such an important part in Evon's life, he obtained an education in music and became a music specialist. He then became the pastor of a church and led its music. Later, he became an itinerant preacher and moved from place to place organizing churches. Throughout his travels, Evon and his family lived in Rubtosvsk, Omsk and Tatarsk, three cities all west of Novosibirsk. While in Tatarsk, he led an orchestra. However, in 1935, unpleasant things began to happen.

Authorities began following all of the believers in Tatarsk, no matter what their faith. It was during this time the NKVD (*Black Raven*) arrested Evon. After he had been in prison for two months, the authorities released him. Maria Vacillovna, Evon's sister, used the connections she had through her husband to get him released. (Maria's husband was the chief of the railway of the Omsk Region during this time.)

Evon's daughter, Luba, heard him coming home at nighttime. She woke up and said, "Father is coming." The family did not believe her words; however, they were very delighted when they saw he had returned. Since he was free again, he often spent a lot of time with his children and his music. His son, Vacilly, and he played the guitar, violin and mandolin together on many occasions.

One evening in late October of 1937, there was a loud knock at the door. Evon and his family heard the noise of the black van outside and Luba became afraid. In fact, all six of the children (now ages 6-17) were afraid, and everyone had trouble sleeping. The NKVD (*Black Raven*) entered their home and examined the books in the family's large library. The authorities put some books into one section, and threw the rest all over the house. The NKVD (*Black Raven*) took most of the books. They also took other items that they found and liked.

Evon knew the men were there to arrest him and asked permission to say goodbye to his children; they did not allow it. Instead, the children ran to him, kissed him, hugged him and cried very loudly as he left. As the men took Evon away, he held tightly to the few things Anna gave him while the men looked at the books. The family did not know why he had been arrested and, unfortunately, they never heard from him again.

After Evon was arrested, Anna and her children had a difficult time, but they survived. Anna cried the whole night after Evon was taken. She even became so sick she could not work. At school, life was difficult for his children too. The children were told they were offspring of the 'enemy of the people.' One day the children were late because their aunt had come to visit and they did not leave for school on time. The teacher mocked Evon's children in front of the whole class. She said, "Maybe these children made a cake and will celebrate Easter and other festivals in the church." As she mocked them, she also scolded them and said, "I will dictate and everyone will write that these children came late and were late because they went to the church." To this day, Vasa and Luba remember the tears that fell onto their papers as they wrote those words.

Luba, Evon's oldest daughter, was 16 years old and had to work in a village 7 kilometers (4 ½ miles) away to support the family. She organized the adults and taught them. Luba also helped at home with the younger children while her mother was ill. Eventually, Luba graduated from school and became a teacher. She started a course for adults following in the steps of her father.

Evon's family wrote many letters following his arrest, but no good word came. They did, however, receive a paper that alleged he was not among the dead. This paper helped to ease the stress on the family some. The Russian government considered the following to be rehabilitation for its people. Usually the paper stated that the person was not proved to be guilty and the government gave a few small benefits to that person and/or his family. The benefit in one case was free transportation and half price on all medications. It would be many years, sometime in 1991, when the family finally received documents telling about Evon's benefits. Evon was found not guilty and his case was closed. His family finally had the documents they needed to prove his innocence when information was requested for official purposes.

During our interview, Lucy shared some things about her grandfather. Evon had been sent to work in a coal mine after he graduated from school in Kiselevsk, located in the Kemerovo Oblast. During WWII, he was called up to fight in the army; however, because he had an ulcer on his leg from when he worked in the mine, he could no longer walk. Therefore, he was put into the hospital. While there, his troop was bombed and everyone was killed. God had protected Evon. After this, he was sent to another place where he was responsible for writing documents for the soldiers. He received this job because he was very clever and had studied for 10 years in school. After the war, he worked in the mine again. This time he made sketches for the mine.

When he was able to return to the church, the NKVD (*Black Raven*) talked with him. Several times, Evon was invited to talk with them because they wanted him to be an informer. They gave him time to think, but he refused and then left for Novosibirsk. For years, he had kept dairies of his activities. However, because of these talks, he returned to Tatarsk and burned all of them. The men invited him again to be an informer but he said, "I will plant your potatoes, but never inform for you."

Before we concluded my interview, Luba, Evon's oldest daughter, remembered a time when one of the members of the communist party came to church; and for what reason Luba did not know. He was Latvian and could have been a spy. He did not come to church all the time, but they thought that maybe he wanted to know God. The NKVD (*Black Raven*) told him he would be promoted in another city; but instead, they shot him. One day, this man's wife came to Anna and asked, "Did you know that my husband was shot? I want to have a rope to hang myself." Anna started to calm her, but the woman refused. She then left and hanged herself. The 7-year-old son of these parents was now an orphan.

The time we spent in Lucy and Luba's home was very profitable. Lucy and her husband are now leaders of the Baptist church that meets in the seminary at Akadem Gorodoc. They also freely shared the struggles their family faced under communism.

Tatiana Gregorivna

It was another very lovely morning in March 2005. Tamara and I met at the River Station metro in

Novosibirsk and took a van to the countryside home of her mother, Tatiana Gregorivna. Tatiana lived on the main road to Academ City (Akadem Gorodoc), the big scientific university in Novosibirsk. Academ City (Akadem Gorodoc) was started during the days of communism as a way for the young Russian minds to work on nuclear research.

After a 30-minute drive, we made our way down a very dusty road to Tatiana's house. She lived in a very clean and large house. Tatiana lived alone, but had many photographs on the walls and many memories of all the years that had slipped by. She had a disability that made speaking and the use of her hands quite difficult.

Tatiana's family lived in Byelorussia until 1930. Her mother was from the Vitebsk Region and her father from Minsk, the capitol of Byelorussia. When Tatiana was nine years old, and her husband was 20, their families were separately visited by the *Black Raven* and sent to exile.

Years later, a house was sold as part of an estate sale. The owner was selling the house because she had gotten herself into debt by playing cards. Tatiana's father, and his brother, obtained a loan and purchased the house that included forests, fields and ponds. All seven ponds had a special purpose. One pond was used for swimming, one for bathing, one for the cows, one for the ducks, one for fishing, one for the sheep and one for the chickens. The house also had very nicely arranged bushes, roses and little paths.

Tatiana's father and his brother paid the loan back in portions. Just after they paid the last note, which gave them full ownership of the property, the government began taking the possessions of prosperous people in small countryside settlements. On Easter Sunday, in 1930, while Tatiana's family ate dinner, the NKVD (*Black Raven*) arrived and told them to get ready to leave. The adults were also told to take the children because they would not return to this place.

The family, which was now considered *kulaks*, gave up everything. Their attractive house and property became occupied by one of the alcoholic local rulers.

They also lost the five cows, horses, pigs, chickens, ducks, sheep and food they had stored in the basement. Everything you would find on the farm that a family needed to enjoy life in those days was now gone. Nevertheless, the NKVD gave the family time to prepare some food and a few changes of clothing for their long journey. While the family packed, Tatiana's father took the fat back from the cellar and cut it into thin pieces. (The fat back is the white meat found on the belly of the pig that Russians like very much.) He arranged the meat around his waist so the authorities would not see it and take it from them.

Tatiana's family traveled with several other families on a train to a small town west of VladiVostok, in the Oboe d'amor. For one month, the families rode in a locomotive freight train that required coal or wood and carried cattle, machinery and wood. There was a toilet in the corner of the car, and the odor was horrible. Tatiana's family ate the fat back, some bread and water; however, there was no additional food, or money to purchase food along the way, so they were very hungry. The families could get water when the train stopped to discharge its freight, but overall, it was a miserable journey. Along the way, families also had to purchase tools so they could work in their new location.

When they finally reached their destination, Tatiana's family found the area was a deep pine forest with no houses or anything else. Her family needed shelter. The quickest way was to dig out a place in the ground. They cut down trees and built a house that was half underground and half above ground called a Zemlanko.

The government had sent Tatiana's family, along with the other families, to this area to pan for gold. They worked very hard, and received only a small amount of food as payment. The families survived on mushrooms and berries from the forest, but were not allowed to have guns or the instruments necessary to hunt game.

Before exile, they had good property because they worked hard. As a result, they were the most qualified to succeed under very difficult circumstances. Later on, they even had a better life than those who forced them to leave their native land. The people in exile shared everything with each other and did everything together with joy and great enthusiasm.

Tatiana's father was very energetic, outgoing, and active. He also enjoyed singing. The one good thing about being in exile was that the young people were not called to join the Soviet Army when the war started in 1941. They were considered 'enemies of the people.'

In 1975, Tatiana's family left the place where they were living. An artificial lake was going to be dug in the area where their house and village currently sat. Her family received 300 rubles for their house. This was equivalent to four to five months of salary for one person. The family was told they could move anywhere they liked in Russia. Therefore, they moved to Novosibirsk and purchased a house near Academ City (Akadem Gorodoc) for 8,000 rubles. Tatiana's father bought two cows for his wife and four daughters. He also got a job as a lathe operator and Tatiana worked in a store that sold clothes, food and other things in a small town.

Zenia and His Relatives

One lovely Sunday afternoon in March 2005, I was visiting my very good friends, Bob and Iris Piatt, at their apartment in north Novosibirsk. They are senior missionaries with the Grace Brethren Mission and continue to be a great encouragement to me. We often had a meal together at Christmas and Thanksgiving where Bob was always the life of the party. One day, Bob reminded me he had a young man in his church, Zenia, who had an interesting story.

Zenia was a teacher with impeccable English and took time to ponder and carefully choose just the right English words to convey what he felt in his heart. He taught English to students in a one-on-one tutor format. He was 38 years old and single. Zenia began his story by telling me that during WWII, Stalin made a law that required soldiers to drink 100 grams of 96% proof liquor before going into battle. Stalin believed drinking made the young men brave as they fought for their motherland. He said, "This is when Russia began to drink heavily as a country."

At the young age of 14, Zenia experienced the negative effects of alcohol. One weekend, Zenia's father, and the father of Zenia's classmate, drank heavily as they celebrated the birthday of Zenia's father. Zenia went to bed, and the next morning his classmate's dad was dead. It is important to understand that this death affected Zenia very deeply. Just one month later, a Baptist friend helped Zenia understand the gospel. He repented of his sins and came to faith in Christ in 1992. God brought a major change in his life during that time.

While in college, Zenia worked the night shift in a morgue. It was here that he also experienced the negative impact alcohol was having on his community and country. As the dead bodies arrived, he noticed the people were mostly men between the ages of 30 and 50. The cause of death was usually related to alcohol or suicide; quite a few of the suicides resulted from drinking.

Zenia's story continued with a discussion about Nicolai, his grandfather. Nicolai was born in 1910 and began working as a shepherd's aide at the age of six. He later became the head of a collective farm in Altai, a region about four hours south of Novosibirsk. When Nicolai took over the farm, it was almost bankrupt. Nevertheless, he worked very hard and made the farm a success. All of the work was very specialized and every person had a specific job to do. Some people milked the cows, some shoveled manure, some prepared the soil, and some planted.

At night, the people on the farm read books or the newspaper for entertainment. Through their reading, they learned of Khrushchev's new law. The law stated that each family could have only one cow, regardless of the number of children in the home. Khrushchev told everyone with two cows to take one cow to the collective farm and they would receive some money for it. In the mornings, a cowboy drove the cows owned by private individuals out to graze and someone drove the bull from the collective farm to breed these cows.

Zenia's grandmother also encountered difficulties with communism. One day, while she worked as the manager of a store, the NKVD (*Black Raven*) found 12 rubles extra in the cash register. She was sent to prison for one year for this crime. Her actions were seen as a scheme to steal from the people and put it into her own pocket. During these days, the value of the 12 rubles was six loaves of bread.

Upon my return to the states, and before I left for another journey back to Russia to do further research, I received the letter from Bob notifying me that Zenia had died of a heart attack. His death surprised and saddened me very much. I felt Zenia's death perhaps revealed the very poor health that many Russians still experience today because of poor diet and the pollution in both the water and air. Zenia's death was even more devastating to Bob because he was grooming Zenia to become the leader of the church that meets in his house each Sunday. It was a joy to know Zenia and learn through our interview that he was a fellow brother in Christ.

Trefon and His Family

During 1937, religion was forbidden; however, Trefon continued to work as an Orthodox priest in Linenkusnets, which is 100 miles east of Novosibirsk. Stalin's henchmen killed him and his son. These men believed Trefon and his son represented the intelligentsia and were 'enemies of the people.' The intelligentsia was the educated people of Russia.

Sometime in that same year, Trefon's other son, who was also Tamara's father, was arrested and sentenced to 10 years. The authorities alleged he too was part of this intelligentsia. When Tamara's father was sent to prison, she was eight years old and her brother was seven months old.

Times were very challenging for the family. Tamara's mother, Varvara, wanted to teach school, but was kicked out because she was considered a part of the 'enemy of the people.' In addition, the people of their community did not talk to each other on the street because they feared the government officials. Even the children did not play together on the streets for two years. Tamara and her family were also removed from their apartment and had to live with relatives in a small, one-room dirt house that was 90 % underground. They now had no money, so they sold furniture, jewelry and other things so they could purchase food to feed only the children.

After two years, Varvara returned to her work as a teacher, and after 10 years, Tamara's father returned home. By this time, his health was very bad. Life in prison was very hard and the poor diet and cold weather took their tolls on him. When he returned home, his feet were so bad they had to be amputated. As part of his rehabilitation from this surgery, he received a two-room apartment and a wheelchair from the government.

Ola's Family

Ola grew up in a small town west of Novosibirsk. Her father was the principal of the school. He instilled very wholesome values in his children through the way he lived his life and taught his children. He did not drink, smoke or participate in negative behavior or language.

Ola's father was a strong Orthodox believer and an example in their community. He tried joining the army on two different occasions, but was deferred both times. Ola's father rejected those deferrals and left for the war anyways. He became a major in the army and was killed near the end of the war.

Ola's family lived in one room. At night, her mother and the three girls slept on the very narrow bed, while her brother slept on the floor. The girls slept with their head and feet staggered, which gave each female adequate space. In Russian, this sleeping style is called *valletta*, which means the feet of one person are at one end and the head of another at that same end.

During the war years, Ola, her two sisters and one brother were hungry. Everyday she went to school without breakfast. Every night, Ola's mother said, "What will I do to feed my family tomorrow?"

Daily, Ola and her siblings took turns saving a place in the bread line. They stood in line all-night and waited for their mother to arrive at 6 a.m. When Ola's mother arrived, she waited for two hours until the store opened . This was when she could use her card to get the daily loaf of bread for her family. The line of people was very, very long and everyone was very determined to get their bread because they had waited so long for it. Some people were even ready to fight for their bread, but were afraid to for fear the authorities would punish them. Once Ola's mother arrived at home, the family ate all of the bread because they were so hungry.

Several weeks later, Ola's brother found some potato peels that had been thrown out near the train station. He gathered them up, took them home and the mother made potato soup from the peels.

One day, her mother brought home 2 kilos of flour and made some wonderful bread with it. It was so good. The flour was sent from America and Ola said, "Now you know why I love Americans. They saved my life." For the first ten years of Ola's life, she was hungry, even though she was the child of an army officer.

As Ola talked about her childhood and the hunger she experienced, she told me about one occasion when she played under a table with a long tablecloth at a neighborhood playmate's home. The child's mother had made pies and the aroma drove Ola out of her mind because she was hungry. Her friend's mother gave a piece of pie to her daughter, but did not offer one to Ola. Ola saw the pie and asked her friend if she could have a bite. The friend allowed her one; she took such a large bite, that Ola bit the girl's finger. The child screamed. Ola was so embarrassed, she ran out of the neighbor's house.

It was in the 1950's that Ola's older sister, Laura, began working in the school as a secretary at the age of 13. She was very good at writing documents. This was an excellent skill since there were no typewriters. Laura was very kind, merciful, wise and played the role of our father as well. She used the money she earned to support the family and everyone liked her very much.

On a regular basis, Laura went to dances. One day, she met a boy who was much older than she and she fell in love with him. This boy, Tim, was the only photographer in their small town of Kupina, located in western Novosibirsk County. He had beautiful blue eyes, nice white skin, and was a rich, young Polish man. To the contrary, Laura had curly blonde hair, hazel eyes and very smooth skin like her mother.

The night Laura and Tim met, she wore a new pair of high heels and a silk dress that was green with white strips. When she walked, she carried herself like an American girl; but trouble awaited her. The tragedy was, Tim was sick with tuberculosis; which is very contagious. No one in Laura's family knew Tim was sick, except maybe Laura's mother. After every meal, Ola's mother washed Tim's dishes with soup and plenty of scalding water as a protection against the disease.

One time Tim's boots leaked, causing his feet to get wet. This caused his tuberculosis to become even worse. He frequently coughed; however, he was still made the provider, or the *carmella* in Russian. He brought home meat, birds, ducks and other animals from his hunting expeditions in the swamps. Because of Tim's disease, and the family's continuous exposure to him, it became a very dangerous time for the family.

When Laura and Tim were still very young, they married and were given a kitchen and a room with two beds. Ola's mother, Ola and her other sister slept in one room, while Laura and Tim slept in a corner. Ola's brother slept behind the stove in a little corner of the kitchen. His bed was a wooden table, or *topchun*, that sat behind the stove. Because everyone slept staggered in the beds, it protected Laura from contracting Tim's tuberculosis. Ola said, "Now I see how great God was in how he kept all of us from getting sick like Tim."

One day, Ola returned from school to find Laura at home alone and lying on the bed very pale and crying. Laura said, very respectfully, "Olictka, sit by me," so she did. The word *olichka* is a very personal, affectionate way to speak a girl's name in Russian. "Take this and throw it in the toilet" Laura said. She handed Ola something wrapped in a cloth that felt a little heavy. Laura repeated, "Take this and throw it in the toilet, and do not let anyone see you doing it."

As Ola threw the bundle into the outhouse, she saw what was a little baby boy that was approximately four months in age. His red, bloody body had a little nose and big ears. At that moment, Ola did not know how she could live because it was so awful and terrible to that little baby there in the toilet. She wanted to throw herself into that hole and retrieve that baby, but he was already dead. As she gasped with her hand on her chest, she said, "I did not know what to do because this deed is forever and it cannot be changed."

Ola slowly returned home, crawled onto the bed and cried with Laura. Even though she was only 10 years old, felt sorrow and mercy in her heart. She also knew Laura had suffered while she had this abortion. Laura had the abortion because a doctor told her the baby would have tuberculosis and she would have it too. She lay on the bed in great pain, dying on the inside. Laura loved her little son, but chose to abandon him due to circumstances. Laura and Ola carried this secret with them throughout the rest of their lives.

At the age of 13, Ola found the family's encyclopedia and read about child bearing. She did not know why or how some girls could not bear children. She read that if the bones at the top of the shoulders are unhealthy, then a girl could not bear a child. It was at that moment she felt something pull in her shoulder and it made her very depressed. She could not believe that she would not bear children. When she was 19, the Lord told Ola that she would not have children. It happened one day when she saw a pregnant woman. She said, "Lord, I don't want to look like that." Ola said the Lord's reply was, "Ok, you will not have children." At the time, she was not a believer and could not remember how God spoke to her, but she knows he did. Coincidently, she never had children.

Sometime after Laura had the abortion, she ran away from Tim to an aunt's house in Novosibirsk. He looked for her, but never found her. He later died at age 27; all of his sisters and brother also died in their twenties due to tuberculosis. Laura remained hidden from Tim and studied in the institute. She eventually married again and had several children. She became very successful in business. She was also blessed to have a husband and mother-in-law that were very good to her.

Ultimately, Laura became the chief in a large trading company. Her son married and he and his wife had two daughters. This son is now the chief at the railway station in Novosibirsk. Laura's two granddaughters studied in the universities and received very good marks on all their tests. She now had a healthy and wealthy family, which was a dramatic change from her life with Tim. She also continued her great friendship with her sister Ola. (Their friendship was enhanced because of the secret they shared). They often saw each other on the weekends and went skiing, talked, went to the forest, went to the cinema and worked in Laura's summer garden.

On one occasion, Laura prepared a large table for guests at one of her birthday parties; however, she did not invite her mother because she still blamed her for letting Tim come into their home knowing he was sick. (Birthday parties are very important to the Russian people!) Ola's mother asked that these final words be delivered to her daughter. She said, "Tell Laura that maybe in this life you cannot understand what I did by letting Tim come into our home, but maybe in the future, somehow you will understand." She also said, "Tell Laura that I love her." In the end, Laura blamed her mother for her abortion, and her mother was offended that Laura would blame her for this. Unfortunately, they parted without forgiving one another. Both have now passed away.

During Laura's final days, she went to church with Ola, repented and was baptized. Laura went to Bible studies and times of worship, and in her final prayer, she remembered that she had not been reconciled with her mother. Laura has since passed away. Ola still occasionally goes to the cemetery and speaks over Laura's grave, prays for her and reminisces about their secret, which now only she carries. Ola closed by saying, "That is my story."

Alexander Stephanovich

The weather in Siberia changes very quickly and is known for being cold. Even on summer's hottest days, it felt cold when the wind blew. My hands experienced this cold as I took a brief 13-minute walk to the metro station. I rode the metro to the end of its line where I got off and began a 10-minute walk to the Chovcheck (ark referring to Noah's Ark) House of Prayer.

When I arrived, I rang the bell. An elderly, and somewhat bent forward man let me in. His name was Alexander Stephanovich, or better known as Brother Sasha. He unlocked the front door to the new church building, led me into his small bedroom and explained that he wanted to name the church after Noah's Ark.

Alexander was born in 1927 in the Altai Region. This was south of Novosibirsk in a village called Berrygrove. His parents were Orthodox believers and his father worked caring for horses. Even though they were poor, he attended school and finished the seventh grade. In 1937, his family moved north to Novosibirsk.

It was in Novosibirsk that his father worked as a street cleaner and had a second job as a guard. Sasha's mother worked in construction recording the loading of heavy wooden boxes. At the age of 12, Sasha began working in a factory that made snow skis. While working, he contracted typhus. It was caused by a lack of vitamins in his diet and the lice that were found in his hair. Often he said, "But God saved me and I survived."

While he was experiencing these health problems, a neighbor who was a believer challenged him to pray about his problems. It was during this time he become a believer. He thought about his parents being Christians and he knew his father was Orthodox. His mother was of the 'old faith' so he repented and trusted in Christ.

After he was well again, he began studying at a flying school. He did not like flying and felt it would be better to stay on the ground and not go up in the air. The aircraft factory was divided into groups. A famous engineer named Antonove led his group. This engineer named planes after himself such as the An-2.

When Sasha became a believer, people asked him how he repented. They raised this question because the moral rules of the young communist league, Consumole, were the same as Christianity. Because he did not understand the rules of the Consumole, he was kicked out of the young communist league. The result was a lower class job in the factory and less pay. As he grew in his faith, he began to share with different people. One group asked him to come and share his new faith with them which he did. He discovered that all of the group members were from a section of the NKVD (*Black Raven*). At this point, he was arrested. Documents were made stating Sasha was a propaganderist, attended the House of Prayer and witnessed to people. The group also tried to accuse him of spying.

Four men, who were all believers, were arrested that day. Two men received 25 years in prison. Sasha and the other man received 10 years. Members of the NKVD (*Black Raven*) took Sasha and the other men by train to Magadon Magadan, located in the Magadan Oblast in northeast Russia not far from Alaska. The train car in which they rode was made of steel and was very cold. It had compartments, but there were no doors on the compartments. The guards controlled the toilets and allowed prisons only one trip to the toilet per day. When they were allowed to use the toilet, they had to run to and from it.

From Magadan, they went by ship to Port Vanena to the Kolyma prison. The ship had 5,000 people in it. Prisoners slept in bunks stacked three high. Sasha had a top bunk. Their food consisted of only salted fish and bread. Prisoners had been arrested for both political and criminal acts. The living conditions on the ship were horrible. Some of the criminals ate the salted fish, not remembering it would make them thirsty. On the second day, these prisoners tried to get some water from a hose that was hanging down below the decks. As the ship rolled back and forth, the men could only take in small amounts of water. As a storm raged outside, the men spilled water on the floor because they had no containers. Because the men were thirsty, they used their caps and smelly shoes to pick up water and drank the water from these items. A number of these men got sick and died because of their great need for water. The guards did not want to be punished because their prisoners had died so they tied the dead bodies to the deck above so they could be counted.

Before going to the camp in Port Vanena, the guards sent the prisoners to the very hot *banya* to kill any lice or diseases. This was done because it was a problem in the camp. The prisoners also received warmer clothes because it was very cold. Finally, the men were taken to the camp, known as Berlag.

Bedeya was Stalin's henchman. He signed the documents for imprisonments. The Russian word for a camp is *lahgear*. If you combine the first portion of each word, it creates Berlag. As they entered the camp, the camp leaders mocked and beat the prisoners. Some of the beatings were merciless, and even resulted in death. Sasha associated his survival with God's strength.

After the Berlag Camp, Sasha was transferred to still another camp known as Kolyma. While in this camp, Sasha was worked in a cobalt mine that was about 3,000 feet deep. The workers would get into a large steel bucket, were lowered down into the mine and began to work. The walls of the shaft walls were frozen because of the extreme cold. Outside of the mine, it was negative 40 degrees centigrade. Inside, it was 22 degrees Fahrenheit. When there was no electricity, they used the lights on their hats. When the batteries were too weak, they used their torches to find their way. If the electricity was still out at the end of the day, a windlass was used to hoist them up.

Sasha used drills and dynamite to break loose and remove the cobalt. The work was seven days a week and 10 hours per day. There was either no lunch or very little because the guards would not draw them up for lunch. Sometimes, they might have a little bread or salted fish for lunch; however, most of the time the men only received breakfast and supper. It was always very cold and the boots were made of wool called *valinky*. This material was similar to the hoofs of mules. The outside of the boots was made of a material similar to horse or goat hair. Sasha did say they were very, very warm. One day, the prison needed someone to work on the lathe. Sasha, who had developed heart and lung problems while working in the mine, volunteered because earlier he had been a steel worker. He feels this machine job helped him survive.

When the prisoners were needed for work outside of the camp, the guards would treat them differently. They would require the prisoners to lie down on the ground and would scare the men by firing the weapons over their heads. The men tried to crawl and run away while the guards had their fun. The prisoners agreed that even the Germans were not as cruel as these guards. The men knew the Germans were cruel, but these Russian guards, and especially the Jewish guards, were both cruel and satanic in their treatment of the prisoners. The guards strongly believed that everyone there was an 'enemy of the people.' Therefore, they poured punishment on these men and women prisoners just to continue satisfying their sadistic desires.

Kolyma prison is known as the worst prison in the string of prisons scattered all over Russia at that time.

The food at Kolyma was not too bad; however, the amount they received was not enough for working men who were required to meet a certain quota each day. The guards feared they would be killed if they went down into the mine. Therefore, if a man did not meet his daily quota, he did not receive supper. Everything was a control issue. They were limited to 800 grams of bread per day and two spoons of porridge, or oatmeal. Each man received a very small amount of sugar for his tea and there was no meat. Sometimes the soup would have a fish flavor. The cooks would put a sack of fish into the big pot. After some time, they would remove both the sack and the fish. This sack was called a misket, and you can guess who ate the fish.

The men slept in one of seven barracks. It was here that Sasha found joy in fellowshipping with two other brothers in Christ. One of the men in Sasha's barrack was a criminal from Estonia. He had tried to escape from the prison in his homeland but was caught. He was sentenced to 10 years of hard labor in Kolyma. While there, Sasha and his friends had the privilege of leading him to Christ.

Life with criminals in a prison camp was a large stress with which Sasha and his friends had to contend. The criminals raped some of the women prisoners and defied the guards. They did receive punishment and some even died at the hands of those guards. I got the feeling that Sasha did not tell me half of the horrible things that went on in that prison.

The prisoners in Kolyma came from a number of different nationalities: Germans, Latvians, Estonians and many others. When these men met to fellowship and pray, they did it secretly. There was a guard tower on every corner of the compound. Therefore, when Sasha and his friends found moments to talk and pray together, they watched in every direction. If they saw the guard coming, they would disperse. One plan they carried out was to stand in line in front of the toilet and pretend to be waiting. They would move very slowly through the line to give more time for prayer and fellowship. Sasha said, "God blessed us."

One day they met a sister in Christ who worked in the prison. She was not a political prisoner. This woman worked for pay and signed all the work documents. Sasha and his friends began talking with this woman and she discovered they had no Bible. She was able to smuggle a little New Testament to Sasha. He hid it in his mitten as he was coming out of the mine; however, he was caught with it as he returned to work.

Sasha was taken to the director and was asked how he got this Bible. He said, "God gave me this little Bible." The director responded with "How?" "I found it on the ground," said Sasha. As punishment, he was taken from the mine and put to work in the kitchen. He had no experience with food preparation. His task was to open cans of stewed meat from America. After only one month, praise God, his Bible was returned.

The Estonian prisoner that Sasha had helped lead to Christ could not read so Sasha taught him to read the New Testament. After this man was released, he returned to Estonia and became a pastor. He started two churches in Tallinn and invited Sasha to visit after he was released. He continued as a pastor until his death in 2003.

In 1956, Sasha was released from Kolyma and his health was very poor. In fact, it was so poor he could not walk due to the cold, poor diet and hard work he endured. He was sent back to Magadan and it was there that some fellow believers helped him. Sasha was required to stay in Magadan for three years and could not go beyond 101 kilometers (about 60 miles) from the city. Once a month, for all three years, he had to report to the authorities. While traveling the 101 kilometers, he found some believers. The authorities opposed him doing this.

During his required stay in Magadan, he received word from Novosibirsk that a very close relative was sick, dying and that he needed to come home. The chief allowed him to return. Once Sasha left Magadan, he never returned. The fellow believers in Magadan gathered money so Sasha could purchase tickets for his trip home by both ship and train. When he arrived in Novosibirsk, he had no documents showing he was free and available for work. Employers were also unwilling to hire him because of his background as a political prisoner. Eventually, he did find employment.

It was at Kamenskaya, a church located in the center of the city, that Sasha met Zahn who later became his wife. He accepted the invitation of his prison friend to go to Tallinn, Estonia. Sasha and Zahn were invited to stay in Tallinn and work but he needed to know if God wanted them to stay. He said if they could find a flat on the second floor of a building, they would stay. Flats were found on both the first and third floors, but not on the second. This was their answer from God and they returned to Novosibirsk.

He preached to the young people in Novosibirsk and some came to Christ. Because of a great need among the hearing impaired, Sasha and Zahn started a church for them. They first met in a cinema and as many as 200 people came to view the Jesus film. Over the years, God prompted many people from numerous countries to come, work and give money to purchase materials to build a House of Prayer for the hearing impaired.

Over a 10-year period, much hard work went into the building of this church. A team of two men and one woman came from Michigan to work on the building. Dick, Jerry and Martha were willing to move dirt using a two-man dirt container with handles. Another individual came from Louisiana and completed manual labor. Some German brothers also came. Todd Nance, one of the project's journeymen gave a gift of $800 for building supplies. Sasha and Zahn both trusted God until a beautiful building for worship was erected. Nobody loves a beautiful building more than Russians. According to Zahn, this church for the hearing impaired is the only one of its kind in Russia. Sasha humbly said, "We are only little tools in God's hands to do His work."

Brother Sasha was one of the most humble men I met while in Russia. During the years we served in that country, I visited Sasha's church. He encouraged me many times during those difficult years by simply accepting me as a missionary. That acceptance brought a lot of joy to my heart. As I look back on this interview, I am amazed by the joy in Sasha's heart as he and Zahn told of their ministry to the hearing impaired in Novosibirsk. Currently, there is a young, hearing pastor leading the church and it is doing well. God is to be praised.

Sasha and Zahn did not have any children, but they are deeply loved by the precious brothers and sisters who worship in their church. Brother Sasha and sister Zahn are my heroes.

Alexei Vladimirovich Bulatov and his Maternal Grandmother

Alexei Vladimirovich Bulatov is our good friend from Russia. He was my first tutor when I started learning Russian in July 1993. He was a college professor of Russian literature. He came to our apartment in the western side of Novosibirsk and I paid him $1 per hour of instruction. He was, and still is, an excellent teacher.

As we developed a friendship with Alexei, he told us about his life before he met the Savior. While studying literature in the university, he found a book in the library that had no name on its cover. As he read it, he noticed all of the pronouns were in capitol letters. This amused him. After reading this book, which was the New Testament (some believer had placed it there without a name) and hearing his professor continually tell the students there is no God, he asked, "If there is not God, then why must you constantly tell us that there is no God?" These events prompted Alexei to learn more about Christianity. Ultimately, a fellow believer who worked for an organization known as the Navigators led Alexei to Christ; whereupon, he quickly began growing his new faith.

Ola, Alexei's wife, was unhappy because he began living life differently and they lost their friends. After some time, she got sick and needed medical attention. Since we were friends with Alexei and Ola, we sent prayer requests to our prayer partners asking them to pray for Ola's healing. Some of the prayer partners wrote us letters telling us they were praying for Ola. We gave these letters to Alexei; he took them home and translated them for his wife. She was amazed that American strangers would pray for while her Russian friends did not seem to care about her failing health.

One day, while Dr. Roger Owens was doing missions work with a group in our city, he learned of Ola's illness. He discovered she needed a special series of shots that could only be purchased in the United States of America. The cost was $3,000 for six shots to be given over a 6-month period. By faith, Phyllis and I planned to purchase the medicine for her. Before we could make the purchase, Dr. Owens told us a pharmaceutical company would donate the medicine and have it on his desk Monday morning. Phyllis took the medicine to Novosibirsk and gave it to Alexei. He put it inside his coat to keep it from freezing and through this, God healed Ola. Since her illness, she has trusted Christ as Savior.

Currently, Alexei, Ola and their daughter Dasha are enjoying life very much. They are serving the Lord as directors of the Russian Bible Society of Siberia and selling Bibles to anyone who desires one. They are truly our wonderful friends.

As our friendship grew with Alexei, Phyllis and I learned about one more member in Alexei's family, his grandmother. This dear woman known as *Babushka*, or grandmother in Russian, lived a normal Russian life as a child. Alexei's Babushka was born to poor peasant parents on April 1, 1914 in a small town 130 kilometers

(90 miles) south of the Novosibirsk Region in Siberia. Babushka's father was killed in WW I on June 22, 1917. Her mother raised three children by herself because there were no relatives to help her. There was an uncle, but he was a Prisoner of War (POW). Because her father had been killed, the government gave free land to her family. Neighbors helped her plow the garden where she grew potatoes, carrots and cucumbers. At this time, the collective farm produced wheat, oats and rye. It also planted tobacco and produced tobacco products.

At the age of six, Babushka, the Russian word for grandmother, started in school and continued through the completion of sixth grade. She recalls her teachers were very strict and one was known as the *Wolf*. The children were certainly afraid of this teacher as they studied language, history and physical education. One day the children attended a play at school that taught them about the basics of the economy. The play was called "How to successfully choose a husband," but it was really about how to disobey the law. It was a comedy and Alexei's grandmother played the children's roles because she was so short. In her generation, the children also played folk games, had boyfriends and lived the life of villagers. Life was enjoyable during her teenage years and at age 19 she was chosen to represent her village in the election. She was also given the responsibilities of checking the work of a group of people who did the threshing of wheat and other grains in the collective farm. Later in her life, Babushka was appointed as a bookkeeper and worked hard doing that task. She was to receive a medal for her work, but something happened keeping her from receiving it.

At the same time, the government took cows and horses from the village farmers. These animals were given as gifts to families if they joined the collective farm. Babushka's brother left to avoid joining the farm but her sister did join. Life on the collective farm was difficult. Babushka had no more than five dresses. The barter system was popular during this time, so she sold a pig. This gave her enough money to purchase these dresses. People also exchanged seeds, such as wheat or rye, for money. With this money, they purchased clothes and a few little luxuries, such as salt and pepper. In addition, she worked for her neighbor so she could have milk for the family. Even under these conditions, everyone seemed to be happy.

I leave you with two quite unusual stories about Alexei's parents. One day Alexei's father was standing on a mound of snow beside the train station tracks. He was there with many other people waiting for the train. As a train passed, someone pushed Alexei's father, he fell into the train and his clothes became caught on the train car. The train dragged him to death because he could not disentangle himself. Later in Alexei's life, his mother contracted a very serious ear infection that ultimately took her life. These incidents may seem very strange, but events like these happened in Russia quite frequently.

Evon Trophimovich

On a lovely Sunday afternoon, my interpreter Annya Vlasenko, and I met with Maria to discuss Evon, her father, and his life. Evon Trophimovich was born in 1926 in the village of Tara, which is part of the Omsk Region. Life was very difficult because the village was located in a *balota*, or a swamp. Evon grew up in a large family with seven brothers and sisters. Since most of the families in Tara were large, this meant many of the people were related. The large families, also known as *Clark*, owned the land, lived on it together and owned pigs, horses, cows and chickens. The Clark also worked the land and sold what was left. Since there were no church buildings, the families met in each other's homes.

In 1943, Evon married when both he and his wife were 17 years old. They immediately moved to the city of Omsk in the Omsk Region. It was here that they lived for 17 years as believers, or 'believers of the old faith.' Because Evon was very active in the church, practiced his faith, and was very much against the government, the *Black Raven* arrested him in 1960.

The government officials wore black leather clothes, a black leather cap and drove the black van. His sentence was five years and he was forbidden to hold any gatherings for several years. He left behind four children and one more due at anytime. His wife and all of their children cried as he was taken away to the city of Bodaibo, located in the Irkutsk Oblast. This is now a city of 50,000 people and, by air, is two hours east of Novosibirsk. Because Evon was forbidden to leave exile, his family stayed in Tara for three years. Evon's mother was still living when he was arrested, so she lived with his family. His wife and children could not call him, and it took a very long time for a letter to travel from Tara to Bodaibo.

Life was quite harsh in Bodaibo. The men in exile mined gold for the government and worked outside all the time. There was no rest on the Lord's Day, and absolutely no opportunity for worship. Their boots were made of wool to keep out the cold. Their meals contained very little meat and there was very little sugar for their tea; however, they did have bread. This was an improvement from the conditions in the 1930's and 1940's. The men lived in barracks and were grateful they could come in from the cold to rest at night.

After Evon's mother passed away, his wife sold the house, gave away what little furniture they had and moved the children to Bodaibo. Evon's family rode the train to Irkutsk. They then waited one week for an airplane that would take them the remaining 630 miles. In all, it took Evon's wife and five children two weeks to get to Bodaibo. Evon remained in exile; however, he no longer lived in the camp. After his family arrived, he built for his family a four-room house with a large kitchen. As part of his sentence, he could not leave the city, but he was able to work and earned about 10 rubles per month. While he and his family lived in Bodaibo, three more children were born. To provide milk for this family of ten, he bought a cow. It served the family very well; however, there was no extra milk to sell because of the size of the family. There was enough grass for the cow and they had a large *agarod* behind the house. This garden was a great blessing to this large family as it provided vegetables that kept them alive.

The children attended school and the family was labeled, *blagamole*, which meant a person who prays to God. People watched Evon's family, and would come and ask questions since no church gatherings were allowed. One day in 1976, at 2 a.m., someone burned down the family's house. Everything was destroyed except the Bible and some personal belongings that Evon's wife had thrown out the window. In the midst of this tragedy, they were grateful to God because they still had their backyard garden. Within days, the government stepped in and gave them an apartment; neighbors also helped.

Evon now needed money to purchase enough food for a large family. He worked several jobs and his wife worked in a job where she received 40 rubles per month. The money they earned was enough to buy exactly 10 kilograms of butter. In the summer, the children picked mushrooms and berries in the forest and his wife froze the berries in the cellar for consumption during the winter. Through hard work by all of the family members, their garden, animals and God's blessings, they survived. Later in life, Evon moved his family from Bodaibo to Irkutsk.

As Perestroika was on the horizon, life improved for this family and their future became brighter. Proverbs 6:6 (KJV) says, *"Go to the ant, thou sluggard; consider her ways, and be wise."* Evon's family did just that. They worked hard, were smart and survived because of their strong faith in God.

George Mihailovich Medvedev

My friend Anatoly suggested I go to the museum in Novosibirsk. It was there he said I would find some interesting stories. In June of 2005, another friend named Nina, met me at the back door of the museum and graciously helped me meet the right people. It turned out I had to pay for this information; however, I am grateful to acquire it.

The following story is about a communist man in Novosibirsk who was loyal to his party. The court proceedings you will read about give us a clue about how the laws and courts worked in Russia during those times. In my opinion, the officials had their minds made up about George before they ever began his trial.

George Mihailovich Medvedev was born in 1909 in western Siberia to a middle class peasant family whose father was an active participant in the punitive force. George completed seven years of schooling and then joined the Communist Party in 1929. He was an active worker in Komsomolsk, the Communist Youth League, and held a high position within the party doing work for the Army. In 1931, he was removed from his duties in Komsomolsk and sent to Irkutsk to be an instructor of political work for the NKVD (*Black Raven*) in its People's Commissariat of Internal Affairs, Escort Regiment Number 235. Approximately four years later, he became a member of the Tribunal in Irkutsk. It was there that George worked with documents for the members of the Communist Party and its candidates.

On December 27, 1936, the *Black Raven* struck again. George was arrested, sentenced and sent to a correctional labor camp located in Siberia in Severnaya Dvina. In addition, the investigation was stopped in February of 1937 due to a lack of data supporting George's participation in the organization. From the beginning of February to the beginning of July, he does not recall being taken for an interrogation; and yet, the following is a court report from George's interrogation on February 13, 1937 in Novosibirsk.

Question: "Do you insist that you not tell the truth about the Trophkestskoi activity? The investigation insists on proof."
Answer: "My facts are accurate."

Question: "When, and who, directed you to the post of the librarian in the 16 convoy company?"

Answer: "I was appointed to the library post by the chief of the political department, Obertaller. And [I was] instructed to do work in a company by the instructor of a political department named Denisov."

Question: "The investigation considers your assignment to the librarian post to be improper and you are being removed. Also, we are removing you as secretary of a communist party organization and demoting you to a lower rank by Obertaller because we believe your facts are false."

Answer: "I think the library post was an act of rehabilitation in the 16 convoy company for me. Your accusations against me cannot be proved correct."

George stated he was not guilty and on October 8, 1937, the verdict from the office of the military prosecutor was read. The following report is called the Bill of Particulars and reads as follows:

"In November of 1936, the NKVD (*Black Raven*) revealed and liquidated the counter-revolutionary terrorist organization in the fourth escort division. It had its purpose to overthrow the soviet power and restore capitalism in the country. The organization operated under the direct orders of foreign bodies and was part of the military plot of the Siberian District Military Command. One of its participants is [George Mihailovich] Medvedev who was recruited by one of the heads of the organization called Denissov. The accusation is that Medvedev carried out counter-revolutionary activities using his service position. He kept prohibited literature in the library and spread it among the military men of the military unit.

Medvedev pled guilty to the accusations; therefore, the criminal activities prove to be true by the facts of the accused.

The facts are Dennisov, Oblertaller and the material investigation.

October 9, 1937, the condemnation of Medvedev."

George was condemned by the Military Board of the Supreme Court of the Union of Soviet Socialist Russia to 10 years of imprisonment in a camp. He will have no political rights for five years and his property will be confiscated. George admitted he had been involved in the terrorist organization and was recruited by

Denissov to distribute literature among the Red Army men. This criminal activity proved to be true by the facts of the participants, Oblertaller and Denissov, of the anti-soviet organization who were also condemned. In reality, George was only guilty of not reporting that Denissov was an 'enemy of the people.'

George was released from the correctional labor camp on December 27, 1946. He remained in Severnaya Dvina and became a senior auditor for a financial branch of Sevzheldorlaga, which is the Ministry of Internal Affairs of the USSR. Just two and one half years later, he was arrested again and held in custody in the prison in Arkhangelsk, located in the Krasnoyarsk Region. It was here George worked as a mechanic on electric saws.

On July 11, 1949, just 14 days after his arrest, there was a special meeting to discuss his case at the Ministry of National Security of the USSR, and on August 3, 1949, there was a second meeting. The results of this special meeting were George was sent to exile at a non-changing residence in the remote part of the Soviet Union. After he was in exile here for almost five years, George wrote a letter on June 13, 1954, to the general prosecutor of the USSR. He felt compelled to write this letter because, sometime in 1949, George learned about a document he had signed while in prison OR while being interrogated back in 1937. George remembers reviewing a document, but it was during a time when his mind was unclear. The prison authorities had held him in his cell for more than five days straight before presenting this document to him. At the time, he believed the document was correct; however, after George read it with a clear mind, he realized the facts in the document were awful and ridiculous. George knew at this point, why the authorities had not shown him the report when he was in a sensible state of mind.

His letter read:
> "I ask that you reconsider my application about my verdict of ten years of imprisonment taken out in 1937 and again in 1949 for my exile where I am presently. I doubt that the organization actually existed that was involved in my sentence."

> George concluded his letter with, "But I, for 18 years, have remained a true communist and thus was active. I ask that you give me a chance to again become a full member of our society and I will bring many benefits to our motherland."

On May 9, 1956, the Military Board of the Supreme Court of the USSR held a session.

The main public prosecutor for the military asks the court to cancel George's verdict from October 9, 1937 based on newly revealed circumstances. Secondly, he asked the court to stop the case because of the absence of a crime. His final request was for the court to cancel the decision of the August 3, 1949 Special Meeting at the Ministry of National Security of the USSR. All three motions were based upon material evidence and an additional check showing that George was condemned without foundational facts.

Eremina, the main prosecutor, attached copies of the interrogations of both George and Obertaller to this Obertaller report. It was proven that the facts of this case could not serve as proof of guilt since they were not objective and they were denied based on a lack of evidentiary materials found in an additional investigation. In this new trial, Obertaller claimed Denissov recruited George for the anti-soviet organization and Denissov agreed he knew about George from Obertaller. George's new case did not contain the original reports from the interrogations. Eremina confirmed George was a participant in the organization, but in court he did not verify or prove that true. Therefore, it was not established that George belonged to the anti-soviet organization. His guilt of storing literature in the library of the military unit in 1955 and distributing it was also not established. An additional check of the new facts confirmed George arrived to work in the military unit as a librarian and personally found the Trofkestkoi literature. There was a witness to confirm this information. Finally, on May 26, 1956, the Military Board of the Supreme Court cancelled the verdict from 1937 and the decision of 1949 because there was an absence of any crime.

By the time George's case came up again in court, the country had a different leader and life in Russia had begun to improve. As a result, he was declared free; even though the government never admitted they were wrong in sending him to exile. The report simply states George could not be proven guilty, and therefore, the charges against him were dropped. To this day, the government has never admitted to any wrongdoing. The government believed it was right, regardless of the circumstances. Perhaps, to some degree, all governments still think along those lines.

Kornei Korneiyevich

It was at the Kamenskaya Church that I met brother Anatoly. He told me he could introduce me to Yakov, a man who had a relative that had gone to prison three times. Yakov was a man of about 40 years of age. His house was very neat and orderly. Outside, there was a very nice garden located within the fenced wall and beside his house. Yakov ushered my interpreter, Annya, and me into his study where we conducted our interview.

Yakov proceeded to talk about his father, Kornei Korneiyevich. He was born in 1920 in the Altai Region and had a profound and positive impact on his son's life. Yakov said, "I am what I am today because of my father;" he is currently serving as a second pastor of an unregistered Baptist church in Novosibirsk. Yakov could not remember a single time when his father was guilty of any wrongdoing, even though Kornei was sentenced three times.

The first time Kornei was sentenced, he was accused of not working. He stayed in exile for five years. Before this arrest, he had faithfully worked in the mining industry for 20 years. Kornei was even told he was the only person to receive a special award for his work. The government knew it needed a more solid reason to sentence Kornei to exile; but because he was the pastor of the church, it was difficult. Therefore, they looked into his past and discovered he had been a beggar. This became the excuse for his first arrest.

Before Kornei left for exile, the previously imprisoned villagers formed a circle around him. The crowd shouted at him and accused him of spoiling the people. Even some of the atheists within the group stood up and said Kornei should suffer in prison for the rest of his life while his children lived in an orphanage.

After this, a second circle formed around Kornei that consisted of believers. This circle was so tight; the NKVD (*Black Raven*) could not get to him. That night, he went back into his house and after several days of work, the NKVD (*Black Raven*) arrived again to talk with him. This is when the *Black Raven* came to his work and arrested him. In addition, they would not allow Kornei to go home to say goodbye to his family. Therefore, he left with the clothes on his back in the black Volga. The Volga was a large car made in Russia about the size of a

Buick. Kornei was taken to a remote area 500 kilometers (350 miles) from Novosibirsk in the Kemerovo Region. It was here in Asnike that he would remain in exile for five years. The government allowed his family of seven children to move with him to this village. In total, Kornei and his family lived in Asnike a total of eight years.

Early on, life was difficult, but neighbors gave the family food. Later, when Yakov was 10 years old, Kornei's family purchased their own cow, pigs, chickens and other animals. These years were even more difficult for the family because everyone was against Kornei. They were considered enemies, and at school, the teachers gave lower marks on the tests to Kornei's children because of their faith in God.

While in exile, Kornei worked in the forest cutting down trees and processing the wood. He spent four years in exile and one year later he completed the government's form for rehabilitation. Within Asnike, there was an association of churches and he was chosen to be the coordinator of the work for ten of the churches. While he vigorously did the Lord's work, the authorities became concerned and sought him out again.

About one year after he was released from exile, friends took him to the forest on a motorcycle, left him there and returned to his house. They did not turn on the lights; instead, they talked and prayed for two hours. Those same friends then returned to the forest and took Kornei to Barnaul because the authorities had been searching for him. After one year in Barnaul, a city south of Novosibirsk, Kornei lead a conference for ministers that his wife also attended. It was here that the NKVD (*Black Raven*) came and arrested him again. Kornei's family knew the *Black Raven* was never very far away. Yakov was now 14 and had many questions about why his father experienced such suffering. After this second arrest, school children called Yakov names, said his father was an American spy and his family members were enemies. Nevertheless, as time went on, they made friends and life was much better because people saw how this family lived.

This time, Kornei was sentenced to three years in prison, and not just exile, in the city of Kemerovo. While there, he worked as a builder. Kornei was blessed to have a daughter who attended school in the same city as the prison. On occasion, his daughter went to the prison and looked over the fence for Kornei. She saw her father as he walked to the barracks. It was during this brief encounter that they were able to exchange a few words. One time, she waited five hours for her father. During her wait, some people told her he had fallen and was possibly dead. The believers in the city fasted, prayed and asked God to heal him. The doctors said they did a miracle because no one in such bad condition ever survived. Kornei said, "No, it was God who did the miracle."

Everyone at the prison called him father, but the prison director wanted everyone to be against him. Kornei had a tremendous testimony while in the prison.

At times when men fought, he put his hand on the shoulder of one man and he could not do anything with his hands. The men at the prison wanted an orchestra to play when Kornei was released, but the authorities kept that from happening. They woke Kornei at 5 a.m. and told him to leave immediately so he could not be respected as a hero.

Kornei's third arrest happened in 1988 when he was 65 years old and court proceedings lasted eight days. By this time, his children were adults and had their own families. Kornei was sentenced to four and one half years and lost all of his possessions. The authorities who took his possessions were embarrassed because all he had was a couch, carpet and a radio.

At this prison in Novosibirsk, the prisoners talked and said Kornei would not last more than two years because of his age. His work responsibilities included painting and odd jobs that were not too difficult. Kornei was blessed and was released after just one and one half years. At the time of his release, Mikhail Sergevich Gorbachev — the former Soviet president - was in charge or ruled the country. Things were getting better and Perestroika was just around the corner. God used Gorbachev to help the country get rid of the old Soviet system and move toward rebuilding the country which is the meaning of Perestroika.

Four catastrophes helped President Gorbachev move the country forward. There was a train crash west of the city of Novosibirsk. Our friends were in that crash.

One train was east bound and one was westbound. One was a passenger train and the other a gas tanker train of natural gas. A spark ensued and three tankers exploded like a large bomb. The ashes of the cremated people were gathered up in a small Styrofoam box. Our friends lost two sons in that crash. One tanker obviously was leaking very badly.

Another tragedy was the Armenian earthquake. It is told that one of the Bush sons were there helping the needy people and the TV camera caught a tear flowing down the cheek of perhaps Jeb Bush. Gorbachev said, "That tear did more to remove the cold war between America and Russia than any other thing."

The third event was Chernobyl which was the nuclear reactor that over heated in Russia.

The fourth event was a ferry that capsized killing a lot of people.

Yakov rejoiced when his dad was finally released from prison. Kornei returned to the prison with Bibles. He gave them to the prisoners, asked if they were reading them and answered their questions. During one visit, Kornei was asked if he hated the people who put him in prison. He replied, "Absolutely not." He also said he was praying for them. Whether Kornei was in exile or prison, he remained a strong witness. He kept his spiritual life strong and his family continued holding services in their home while he was away. When he could not preach, he always prayed.

Sometime during 1998, at the age of 78, Kornei died and went to live in his heavenly home, a home he had longed for, for so long. During his life, someone accused Kornei of not loving his family and spending too much time at the church. His response was, "I love my family very much, and the church, but I love God the most with all of my heart." Three of his four sons are currently in some kind of ministry and his three daughters are married to ministers. His life profoundly affected the lives of his children.

While Kornei lived in the Novosibirsk area, he led the underground Baptist churches. The words total commitment come to mind as this man faced his accusers and stayed the course, regardless of all circumstances. I realize that life in Russia is not as difficult now as it was in the days of 1937, 1938 and during the war. However, I am convinced Kornei would have stood strong for his Lord under great persecution, and very likely would have been shot. The legacy Kornei gave his family, even in his old age, showed his love for the Savior. I am sure that prison life at age 65 was not easy, even though the work was not too difficult. An even greater proof of his love for his Lord is seen in how God answered his prayers for his children. Not many families have a family history where so many of the children serve God in their adult lives. The family continues to do so even to this day. We can clearly see that he was a deep man of prayer and obeyed the challenge to put God first in his life. Kornei Korneiyevich is my hero.

Vicelly Simonovich

His name was Vicelly Simonovich and he was born in the Ukraine in 1870. His family worked as farmers in Levov and practiced the Orthodox Christian faith. When Vicelly was eight years old, his parents died during the flu epidemic and left him, a brother and a sister. His aunt assumed the parental responsibilities and raised the children. This chain of events led to Vicelly working on his aunt's farm at a very young age. As he grew older, he decided to work for other farmers to earn money, find a wife and build a house. He liked one farmer in particular because he was such a good boss. He worked for this farmer for 10 years and in return, the farmer gave his daughter, Ann, to be Vicelly's wife. By that time, Vicelly was 30 and Ann was 20.

After they were married, they purchased land and a house. They had three children and soon realized the family did not have enough land. This occurred during a time when the government was reforming the land, so Vicelly and his family was offered free land in Siberia. The government, which at that time was controlled by the Tsar Nickolai II and the prime minister, were giving land to good workers to help internally develop Russia. Before this era, only prisoners lived in Siberia.

Vicelly's family prepared their clothes, tools and free tickets from the government and left on the train for Siberia. Earlier in his life, he earned money in the Ukraine. He decided to put half of it into the Swiss bank and took

30 gold pieces with him to Siberia. A relative tried to obtain the 30 gold pieces from the Swiss bank in the 1970's, but it was useless. The bank claimed there were no records. By 1908, they arrived in the town of Tomsk and found that the government had prepared the land by digging wells. The family came in the springtime and built their house in the summer. During that summer, Vicelly also planted seeds in his gardens and fields.

Within Tomsk, there were virgin forests that contained cones filled with nuts. Vicelly harvested the cones and sold the nuts for money. During the 12 years the family lived in Tomsk, Ann gave birth to two sons. The land was only good for producing rye and Vicelly often had bad harvests, so the family decided to move. He heard there was good land in Novosibirsk. Several people traveled the 270 kilometers (170 miles), looked at the land and found it was better.

The Ukrainian people, who were all known as hard workers, were the only individuals living in Siberia during this time. This did not stop Vicelly from risking it all. He wanted to move to Tomsk, from the Ukraine, and start a new life in Russia. His family asked the government to let them go and work this new land. Permission was granted and they left for Siberia. Plots of land varied in size. The family found that 30-40 acres was good for producing wheat and caring for animals. The temperature would reach negative 65 degrees, but Vicelly's family continued working the new land. Shortly thereafter, Ann gave birth to another son. Vicelly and Ann now had one daughter and five sons. In 1924, Nickolai Lenin died and Joseph Stalin began controlling the government. By 1930, Stalin started the collective farms and required families to give most of their animals to the government. Vicelly had developed a very good farm and was left with only one cow, one sheep, one pig and several chickens. In turn, the director of the collective farm offered a cow, pig or horse as an incentive to anyone who joined the collective farm. One can only guess where these incentive animals came from.

In 1937, all who opposed Stalin were taken to prison. The government gave the poor people power over the rich. During one of the governmental meetings that year, it was decided Vicelly would be arrested next and taken to prison. The NKVD (*Black Raven*) was ravaging the land. They detained Vicelly in a building for one night and by the next day, the city officials decided to take him to prison. However, while he was at the court hearing, the government decided he was honest and just because he always helped poor people. The people of that village rose up and said, "You cannot take him to prison because he has helped all of us when we needed something." If a family needed a way to make a living, Vicelly gave them a horse or a cow. As a result, another man was put into prison and Vicelly was free. After his release, he returned to his farm. For four years, he continued his hard work on the farm.

When Vicelly was 71 years old, WWII began. His sons left to fight in the war and he had to carry on with the farm work himself. Unfortunately, the war had a negative impact on his family. A horse killed one of his children, his son, Vicelly, was killed in the war and all of his other sons were wounded. Throughout Vicelly's life, his formula for success was hard work, devotion to God, positive attitude, wise decisions and a love for people. He always prayed before every meal and honored the Lord with his hard work and eager willingness to help people. God gave him excellent health and he never needed to enter a hospital. He died at the age of 96.

Nicolai and Nina Zezula

Nicolai is the grandson of Vicelly Simonovich. He was a bus driver for his factory for many years, before he retired. Both he and Nina, his wife, remembered life was abundant during Stalin's reign. Crime was low, transportation was very convenient and there was money available for vacations, even several times a year.

When Nicolai and Nina were young, they both worked on the collective farm in northern Novosibirsk County. Nina said they worked everyday in the summer. In the winter, they could rest one or two days only and that was when the brigadier approved it. If they did have a day of rest, they had to prepare all of the feed for the animals before they could begin.

The government placed many restrictions upon the people. Each year, it collected a tax in the form of 100 eggs, 50 kilograms (110 pounds) each of beef and pork, 300 liters of milk and products made from chicken, turkey and sheep. The collective farm did not allow its people to slaughter the animals used to make these animal products. It slaughtered all of the animals for the people and then divided out the meat products. The people were given the heads, tails and feet as their meat products. The government did allow, however, each family to have a small garden behind their house. The families ate the vegetables they grew and it was common for them to have potatoes three times per day.

When Nicolai was 12 years old, he was asked to take food to approximately 50 workers who were 45 kilometers away. He and another boy who was seven, started out one morning. The road was full of holes and this made the pace very slow. He knew that when he reached the muddy river, he was not to cross it. However, when he arrived at the fork where the three rivers came together, it was dark and he could not tell which one to take. As he entered the middle river, he quickly discovered it was the muddy river. When his horse began to swim, he stopped, unhitched the horse from the cart and got the horse and cart out of the river. While all of this happened, the other boy became afraid and started crying. Suddenly, both boys heard another horse and cart coming. It was one of the strong workers, coming to pick up the food. The man hitched both Nicolai's and his horses to the cart with the food and pulled it out of the river. The three chose the river on the right and immediately met the hungry people who had built a bonfire. As the workers saw the cart with food, they sang, "Food, food. It has come." They finished eating the food in just a few minutes because they were very hungry. The boys stayed and slept in the workers' camp that night. The next morning, they ate their bread, which they brought from home, and then began the daylong journey back to their homes.

On another occasion, Nicolai and another boy went to work in another village 40 kilometers away. The boys tired of their work, which was to last one month, so they decided to run away and go back to their homes. When they tried to leave, the chief of the work was walking around the tent. Subsequently, they grabbed their clothes and took off behind the tent. They reached the nearby woods and then had to cross a river. It was at this time that Nicolai discovered the other boy could not swim. He saw two boats on the other side of the river. For that reason, he swam across the river, brought one boat back and helped his friend across the river. The boys now had a 40-kilometer walk ahead of them. They were hot, hungry and somewhat thirsty. The river water was clean, so the boys drank from it and continued. By noon, they were so hot and hungry they lay down on the grass and rested. Sometime in the evening, the boys arrived back at the collective farm and met the director of the farm. As punishment for running away, he took a part of the gardens behind each of their homes away, but he never carried out his threat. It would be at least six more years before Nicolai would meet and marry Nina.

At the age of 16, Nina became friends with the daughter of the collective farm's director. Through that connection, she received a document to go to Novosibirsk to study in the institute. Around this same time, Nicolai also went to Novosibirsk, but he could not get into the institute because he had no documents. Therefore, he went back to the collective farm and worked for two more years. After that, he participated in the army for four years and then returned home. It was in Novosibirsk, at a dance one evening, that Nicolai met and married Nina.

Nina was a lovely young lady age 22 when Nicolai and Nina met at the dance. It was love at first sight. As they began to talk to one another, they discovered that the understanding of each others backgrounds was very unusual. Nicolai and Nina both had worked very hard under the harsh directors of the collective farms. Now they were free from that hard labor and now were strongly attracted to each other. After several months of productive courtship, they joined their lives together in marriage.

Pavel Merkoulovich

Pavel Merkoulovitch was born in 1891 and lived in the Saratovskoy Oblast, southeast of Moscow. In 1917, Pavel and his family worked for a rich man on the collective farm. After the revolution, this man left and went abroad. Before this man left, Pavel purchased some tools and continued working on the collective farm. His family cooperated with their neighbors, worked together and received a decent income. Later, the rich man returned and became the head of the collective farm.

Gregory was the son of the rich farmer. He liked Pavel's daughter very much and diligently pursued her. He even sent a letter to the director of the collective farm about her. In order to avoid Gregory, the family moved to a different collective farm every year for four years. Pavel then gave his daughter's documents to the police and they changed her name. The family was then sent to the Kemerovo Oblast. They traveled in an open train car that had previously been used for transporting cattle. During the trip, Pavel's three-year-old son died. Finally, after at least two weeks, they reached the coal-mining town near Linenkusnets. They moved into this village with no tools or money. They also had no food, so Pavel sent his son out begging for bread for this family of six.

Pavel's family did not have food, but they did have a Bible. All of his family members were good Christian Orthodox people who enjoyed reading the Bible. One day, someone saw their Bible and reported Pavel to the NKVD (*Black Raven*). By 1937, the NKVD (*Black Raven*) arrested Pavel and sent him to the Kolyma Prison, which is west of the Kamchatka Oblast in the extreme northwest part of Russia near Alaska. Upon his arrival, he was interrogated, beaten and killed. Somehow, he sent a message to let his family know he was being accused of trying to blow up a 5-foot wide bridge in Linenkusnets.

In 1961, Pavel's file was discussed by the NKVD (*Black Raven*), and he was rehabilitated after He was declared not guilty of being an enemy of the people. This is when Pavel's wife started receiving a monthly pension of nine rubles. She was grateful for this small amount, even though it was not the average worker's pay of about 80 rubles per month. The government also gave Pavel's family some land. On this land, his family built a house and other people in Linenkusnets saw they were hard workers.

Yakov Feuderovich

Lena was a grandmother I met at a Baptist church in Novosibirsk. She wanted to tell me about her grandfather, Yakov Feuderovich. He was born in 1880 and was the pastor of the Baptist church in the Omsk Oblast. He was short in stature and had a beautiful beard. He was also one of three Christian men who founded the village of *Doebray poli*, which means good field.

During the early 1930's, the NKVD (*Black Raven*) confiscated their home and possessions to make an office. As a result, Yakov and his wife lived in their 6 foot by 10 foot kitchen. It had only a dirt floor and was located in their yard, separate from their house.

In 1937, Yakov was quite sick, confined to a bed and could no longer walk. Lena, even though she was four years old, remembers when the Black Raven arrived at her grandfather's house to arrest him because he was a believer at the age of 57. When they came, Yakov was wearing a white robe, and thank the Lord they did allow him to get dressed. If they had taken him in his robe, he would have died on the way because of not having warm clothing in his sick condition. It was summertime, sometime in June or July, and because he had a fever, the men let him take some warm clothes. In addition, his wife sent with him some pies she had cooked. Yakov's wife was now alone, so she lived in the homes of her grown children and their families. It was sometime later when Lena's uncle wrote a letter asking about Yakov. In return, he received a document that stated Yakov opposed the government and was shot on the third day after his arrest.

Yakov's family members did not give up hope; they just pressed on with their lives.

As you can see, the strength of character of these dear believers revealed how God can strengthen someone and make them a giant for their Lord.

Annya at the Razavet Church

Annya lived in the Smolensk Region and recalled a time when the Fascists moved there. This caused her family to feel cut-off from the rest of the country. The Fascists put the region on a night curfew and restricted everyone's movement by day. No one could leave the region without permission or go to any public place without the watchful eyes of the Fascists. This feeling lasted for one year and resulted in the family being moved to another part of the country. While her family lived in this new area, Annya trained for six months as a manager in a chemical factory. This chemical factory was part of the army's artillery department. In her job, she was a product control representative. If a product was approved, it was sent to the front line during the war. Employees who held this position were required to have a high school diploma and be at least 18 years of age. Annya was only 17 and had finished her schooling only through the seventh grade. Annya believed it was because of God's blessing that she was allowed to work at the main office and hold this job. She held this job for many years and then after WWII ended, she and her parents moved to Novosibirsk.

Annya's recommendation papers for Novosibirsk were good, so her father helped her get a job at the hospital. In her new position, she continued to be an honest and hard worker, just as she had been during the army days. Everything was going very well for Annya until one day between 1946 and 1947, she caught a nurse stealing. She reported this thievery to the authorities. This nurse was upset, and because she was Annya's neighbor, she tried to get revenge. She reported to the authorities that Anya's father was a preacher in the church and held a Bible in his hand while preaching.

People from the political army followed up on this report and went to the church. While there, they saw Anya. The authorities mandated she report to their department, along with the nurse from the hospital.

Since Annya was the secretary for Komsomol, a young communist league that every young person was required to join, her papers were checked and taken by 15 people from the organization. These individuals knew her record keeping was excellent and they did not want to loose a good worker. For the next two weeks, they tried to convince her to denounce her faith. She refused. They even asked her to write an article denouncing her faith. She refused again. She knew her parents had taught her well and that talents came from God. Ultimately, they barred her from Komsomol. Annya immediately gave them her certificate as secretary. The members of Komsomol were shocked that she was so willing to give up this prestigious position. She told them she desired to continue to serve in Komsomol, but would not give up going to the prayer house for worship.

Just as Annya wanted to continue in Komsomol, she desired to continue working at the hospital. A man, however, advised to leave while she still had a good record. Therefore, she left and worked at an engineering factory. Ostenov, a young brother in the church, helped her get this job. During the hiring process, Annya experienced God's mercy again. She was hired in as a third grade worker in her area of specialty. Just one year later, she was promoted to the sixth grade level of work. Her responsibilities included reading engineering drawings. She completed this job just as well as the rest of the workers and as a result received a salary of 165 rubles, half of which was given to her as a pension.

The people under her command were aware that something was different about her and they watched her life very closely. Some individuals were alcoholics, had low character and were lazy. One in particular asked her why she did not curse when she was frustrated. She gave the example of a vessel with water in it. The vessel can contain clean, clear or impure water and when you turn it to one side you can let the clear water pour out. Then you are left with dirt in the bottom. Anya told this individual that her vessel was clean and the people thought of her like a professor who makes things very clear. She took the analogy from her studies of the Bible.

One day while Annya was working at the factory, her boss asked her to cheat on her pension. He wanted her to report more work than she was doing so she could get a larger pension. This was a temptation for her. That night she prayed very hard and then dreamed about two flowers. In her dream she saw, a large cornflower and a big beautiful rose. She stood between the flowers in the factory. A voice came from above which said, "Choose the smaller one because you can put it in your pocket and get your bread." The next day, she told the boss that she would not change the record and would receive the pension that was coming to her. In response to her, he fired her.

God's mercy has carried her throughout her life. Annya knew God was watching over her and said many times, "Only God's mercies." She has clung to her faith regardless of the circumstances and always gave God the glory for His mercy and kindness. While in her 70's, she was very alert and her memory was very good. When she dies and goes to live in heaven, I can see her Savior saying, "Enter into my home Anya, you wonderful, faithful servant. You have been faithful over a few things and now I will put you in charge of greater things."

Victor Vecillovich Near the Razavet Church

Victor Vacillovich was born in 1939 and now lived in a two-story building, near the circus on Obdorlsky Street, in Novosibirsk. When he was 18 years old, he accepted Jesus as his personal Lord and Savior and his heart was on fire. To show his love for the Lord, he went outside and read to the people who crowded around him.

One night, the leaders of the local church held a meeting in which they told the members of the congregation they needed to be like other people and go to the cinema, circus and other public places. In response to this, Victor's father stood up and said that if they act like the nonbelievers, will Jesus accept them? He, and eight other people, left the meeting.

These eight believers now met in the kitchen of Victor's house to drink tea and study the Bible. One day, his neighbors, and even some other believers, reported these meetings to the authorities. As a result, all of the men were arrested and sent to different prisons. One believer had a soft heart toward Victor's father. She made him suits and tried to help him in any way she could while he was in the prison in eastern Novosibirsk.

When Victor was only seven years old, his father was also arrested. The NKVD (*Black Raven*) ransacked their house while they looked for some fragment of a document to accuse his father. Victor cannot remember the details of his father's arrest; however, he knew the NKVD (*Black Raven*) came during the daytime, which was unusual. Victor's family was required to move out of the house for two days while the men searched the house; the family had no place to go.

Since their grandfather was paralyzed, the family took him to a nursing home. Victor's grandmother worked as a nurse in the nursing home so she could care for her husband and the other believers. The authorities continued looking for ways to find even a little bit of evidence that would give them a reason to declare Victor's father an 'enemy of the people.'

Victor's father was now in prison, so his family asked other believers to help them get food for their five children who were all under the age of 10. They went house to house and asked for help, but no one was allowed to help a family of a prisoner. Everyone was frightened because the family had a document that declared Victor's father as an 'enemy of the people.' His children were no longer allowed to go to church, so they quite frequently went to the stadium and watched soccer games. The family now lived in only one room and a kitchen; there was no place for Victor to sleep, so he slept under the bed.

Not everyone denied Victor's family the assistance they needed. One brother in the church, Yevgeni, helped the family by giving them food at night. He also helped in other ways. Another one of the church members bought Victor's family a piece of land in northeastern Novosibirsk. On this land, they built a dugout style house where most of it was underground in the Dzerzhinsky Region. Their *zemlanka* had one window, one door and one chimney. They also built a dugout for a family who experienced the same hardships.

During the imprisonment of Victor's father, no family members were allowed to see him; however, Victor did take food and clothes to him, but had to leave them with the prison authorities. Sometimes he even waited half a day before he could leave the food. On occasion, the other prisoner's dependents asked how to get into the prison; Victor showed them the way. Later, when Victor's family moved to a camp farther away, he sent parcels to his father. Victor's father stayed in prison for seven years and preached while he was there. His preaching resulted in a second term in the camp. Moving to the camp meant he had to leave Novosibirsk where he had lived for two and one half years. Life was more difficult in prison because he had to stay inside, however, the camp allowed him to be outside and to work. While at the camp, he went to court three times to hear his case discussed again by lawyers, and to wait for the sentence from the judge.

At the court, people encouraged Bushmakin, a fellow worker that Victor's father led to Christ when he worked at the railway station, to say that he did not know Victor's father; that is exactly what Bushmakin did. Unfortunately, both Bushmakin and Victor's father were sent to prison. His father received 10 years; Bushmakin received eight years. Fifty years later, Victor's father saw Bushmakin while he was helping build the main Baptist church building in Novosibirsk named Salvation Baptist Church. During their meeting, Bushmakin said the government authorities told him that if he opposed Victor's father, they would free him, but they lied to him.

While Victor's father experienced his challenges, his son grew up and had his own struggles. As a teenager, Victor began to drink and play cards. By 1956, he was 16 years old, so he joined a dance group. The members sang, danced and then drank. Victor's family was concerned about him, so they together and discussed his situation and lifestyle choices. They decided to send him and his grandmother to live with relatives in Achinse, a town near Krasnoyarsk. The day they left, the military came to his house to take him, but Victor was already gone. Earlier, when Victor had been in the military office, a man had asked him about his life. He said, "We know your father stands for good things in prison, and what good will you do while in prison?" To this day, he still remembers that question.

While Victor was in Achinse, he dug trenches and later made deliveries with a horse he was given. After that job, he worked on train engines with his uncle who was an electrician. Due to Victor's behavior, the military continued to look for him. Therefore, he was not free to return to Novosibirsk. The day finally came when Victor returned to Novosibirsk with his uncle. Upon his return, his father, who had just been released from the camp, took a little cart to the bus stop that was four bus stops away to help Victor with his belongings. It had been 10 years since Victor and his father had seen one another. Upon their meeting, Victor's father hugged him and continued to repeat, "My son, my son." It was a very emotional moment for both of them.

After their reunion, Victor went to the church again, repented and was baptized in August of 1958. Less than one year later, at the age of 19, he joined the army and planned to become a pilot until the military leaders learned he was a believer and would not take him. Instead, he became a radio operator, and after six months of training in Novosibirsk, he was sent to another place. Ultimately, he ended up working on scales and was very good at it; therefore, that became his job in the army.

One day, Victor's father learned the military wanted to send him to VladiVostok. Before he left, Victor told his father he would go wherever they sent him. After a year, he joined the troops. One day, someone from the military found an uncovered Bible in his suitcase. When this occurred, Victor was in the kitchen with 50 other men who now knew he was a believer. He told the men he was an electrician and had modernized the radio station. Also in his possession, was the document from when his father was put into prison and his release information. It is intriguing to know this document did not say Victor's father was innocent; it only said he suffered from political oppression and was rehabilitated.

The series of events in Victor's life still deeply affect him. He was fortunate to have a Christian father who loved God and played an active role in his life. Even though his father was gone a lot because of his incarceration, his example and love had a lasting impact on Victor's life and his repentance. Boys who are growing up in Russia today are not so lucky. There is a great need for male Christian role models. I thank God for Christian men in Russia, even though they are very few.

Alexei Iznatchevich in Pestila

Alexei Iznatchevich was born in 1936 in Byelorussia, which is part of the Brest Region. His family was Pentecostal, which meant he began attending church when he was a baby. At the age of 16, his family moved to Novosibirsk. It was here that he met some Baptist brothers; he meant more Pentecostals between 1958 and 1960.

During 1960, Khrushchev signed a new law to have all illegal, or unregistered, churches demolished. At that time, the Pentecostal churches were not registered because the law contradicted God's word. This new law stated that children were forbidden to go to church and the government must place the pastor in the church. Under these conditions, the Pentecostal churches could not accept the law, and therefore, the authorities began to look for these unregistered churches.

One day, both Phillip Evanovich and Alexei went to the police to discuss what the authorities were doing to the churches. The police wanted to keep the men; however, they did not because the men had not committed any crime against the law. A little bit later, an article appeared in the newspaper that criticized the government for being soft on the unregistered churches. As a result, the government reopened Phillip's case, which had been previously closed. Phillip was forced to sign a paper stating he would not leave the area. Six months later, the court convened in the House of Culture regarding Phillip's actions. The government knew this case was a great way to demonstrate what they would do to uncooperative, unregistered churches. The 800 seats in the courthouse were completely filled.

In January of 1961, both Phillip and Alexei appeared in court. Alexei was now 25 years old and unmarried. During these proceedings, the judge sentenced three men and two women, even though they did not have any proof to accuse them. The only information the government had was these five people were trying to get others to join their church by helping them. The court proceedings lasted five days, during which 76 witnesses composed of both believers and nonbelievers testified. The judge gave both Alexei and Phillip a sentence of five years in prison and five years in exile. The women and the other man received a 3-year sentence.

Alexei and Phillip spent their first year in prison in Novosibirsk. Being together allowed them many opportunities to pray together and when the guards saw this, they separated the men and forced them to live in tents. Even under these conditions, they still openly prayed in front of the guards. The guards tried to force them to stop praying again; however, they protested and said the constitution gave them the right to freedom of religion. Consequently, the guards denied Alexei visits with his family members and would not give him the food that they brought for him. (This practice was common during Alexei's incarceration, and still is today.)

While these events took place, both Phillip and Alexei were surprised by the support they received from some of the criminals. The good criminals stood up for these men because of their total commitment to Jesus Christ and their faith in Him. Because these criminals supported Phillip and Alexei, they protected the men from both physical and emotional abuse. Some of the hard-core criminals even supported these believers. They told the other criminals that even though these men prayed, at least they were consistent in their faith and stood up for their beliefs. These hard-core criminals lived by their own principles; but they admired Alexei and Phillip because of their stand for Jesus Christ.

During the period when Alexei was in prison, it was common for prisons to have an isolation cell. It was used to punish rebellious prisoners, and at one point, Alexei was put into it. After his time in isolation, he lived in a very big tent that had a stove for heat. Alexei was placed in the mechanic's group and the guards told the other mechanics to negatively influence Alexei. The other mechanics mocked him for his stand for Christ and were very mean, nasty, hateful and torturous toward him. The mechanics called him Baptist and someone who only prays all the time. Baptists are thought to be a cult by many people of Russia even to this day. Alexei challenged these men to tell him what crime he had committed. He did not oppose the administration of the prison; he only wanted to know why he was in prison and why was he sent to isolation. He tried to help them see that a person could be sent to prison for doing nothing wrong and be punished for no reason. The men were quiet, so he used his example of how the law did not work in his, or their, favor. As a result, he was sent to Krasnoyarsk to a work camp in the wood cutting area because he was influencing other prisoners.

The conditions at the camp were a little better since prisoners could work outside; however, he faced a problem. There were prisoners at the camp who did not want to work for the communist party and opposed the authorities. His work was difficult and required much physical strength, but because of God and his strong faith, he did well. In total, Alexei served three and one half years of his five-year sentence; this was because he had done nothing against his country. Upon his release, he received his document that stated he had been rehabilitated; however, the government never apologized for sending him to prison.

After his release, he returned to his ministry in Novosibirsk. It was here, at the age of 32, that he met and married a Christian woman. The marriage produced two sons and one daughter. Alexei continues to be a very godly and stately man who leads the Pentecostal church in north Novosibirsk. He is 70 years old and he and his wife have the privilege of living with their married daughter. They have 11 grandchildren and all of his family members serve the Lord.

Sergei the Prisoner

One day in 1997, Sergei, a Christian executive, was driving his car in Novosibirsk and was stopped by the police. He thought it was a mistake and that he would soon be let go. Instead, the police handcuffed him and told him they knew what they were doing. They searched his car and made a mess of it, but found nothing. During this search, Sergei asked them what they wanted; they were silent and continued on. In the end, he was jailed for one day and told he was being held for the murder of an executive's wife. He now understood why he was arrested. Sergei had previously worked for this executive as the chief guard of his property. Sergei ended his employment with this rich executive because of a disagreement over his duties. You see, this executive wanted Sergei to kill someone for him; Sergei refused, and as a result, he was being held in jail.

Eventually the police found the real killer, but at the same time, the rich executive conjectured that Sergei could still hurt him and his family. Therefore, the police put Sergei in prison. It took three years for the court to bring his case to trial because the law said that if innocence cannot be established within the first six months of imprisonment, the prisoner must be held longer. Sergei would face three trials, at three separate times, with different people at each trial before he was released.

Overall, there were 30 errors made in his trials. Several people were fired during these times, and even the public prosecutor was fired. The lawyer told Sergei the court must keep a person in prison while they are searching for evidence. In other words, you were guilty until proven innocent. The lawyer also said, "Who will apologize for a moral injury in front of you?"

After several court trials within the first few years, there was still no evidence against Sergei. In each case, there were more errors committed by the judicial system, but they still did not close his case. The investigator even tried to apply any kind of proof to make Sergei guilty. Eventually, the investigator was fired; the high level investigator was fired after that. Other individuals now took over the case. One day, the highest investigator talked with Sergei. This investigator was sure he was innocent, but he could not help him because there were too many people against him. At the same time, Sergei was advised not to admit any guilt; the thought was this would eventually help Sergei.

Three and one half years later, a judge read the long, three-volume case. After three days, witnesses were invited to testify. The witnesses all said Sergei was innocent and that they had never seen him commit any crime. Sergei did not know where these witnesses came from; they did not even know Sergei's name. The people in the court who did know Sergei affirmed his innocence. The prosecutor concluded and the court was delayed for another month. At the next hearing, the judge came in, and without a prosecutor said, "You will have to serve 12 years in prison." The lawyer's papers on Sergei were very positive and reiterated the fact that there was no proof of any guilt.

Sergei had served as a soldier in Afghanistan and received a number of medals. The judge saw this in his case files and it did not matter; this act of service was actually used against him. The judge said that since he used a rifle, it was possible that he could have killed someone. The actual killer also testified and said that Sergei had told him to kill the woman. Later in court, the killer changed his testimony and said Sergei was innocent of the charges against him.

After receiving the 12-year sentence, he appealed to the Supreme Court. This action did not help Sergei because the courts continually changed his information. The first court tried to prove he killed the executive's wife for revenge. The second court, and subsequent courts, changed the facts to suit its taste. At one point, the courts even said he killed the woman for another worker who had been fired by this rich executive. Yet, another attempt tried to make him guilty because he worked for another company and wanted to become its head. Sergei said, "I am not a Robin Hood trying to do things for others like that," because the organization was too complicated for him to become its leader. The Supreme Court also even said at one point he could be declared innocent; but the 12 years sentence still applied. By now, he had already spent four years in prison trying to establish his innocence. Even if he pleaded guilty, they could not change the length of his sentence.

Sergei remained in prison this entire time. The prison conditions before his trials should have been good; however, they were unmitigatingly awful. Since the guards could treat the prisoners in whatever manner they liked, he was treated worse than an animal. His cell was four and one half feet wide and 18 feet long. It was located in the basement with only one very small window. The prison had criminals who lived on the above two stories while the basement was for the hardened criminals. Several of the cells accommodated 500 murderers.

In Sergei's cell, there were 28 men; there were seldom less than that. Eight men slept in one bed; the beds were stacked in tiers that were three high. The prisoners slept on their sides and had to all turn over at the same time. Water regularly leaked down the walls from the ceiling. Bedbugs and cockroaches crawled on the prisoners while they slept. They also had a problem with lice. Just about everyone was sick and only family members were allowed to bring cream to help heal the body. Fortunately, Sergei experienced a miracle and did not get sick. If a prisoner was sick and went to the hospital, he usually died. The bathroom was only one half of a meter and did not have any enclosure. When the men smoked, the smell and fog lingered because there was no vent. The prisoners that lived on the upper two levels, such as the thieves, had better living conditions.

The prison provided one five-minute, hot shower per week. Sergei's wife, Lena, brought soap, clothes and medicine for him, but the guards kept the medicine and would not return it to his wife. For the first two years Sergei was in prison, he was not allowed to see his wife or receive letters from her. Finally, Lena was allowed to visit once a month, during which they talked to one another by telephone through a glass wall.

After four and one half years, there was a 24-hour meeting to discuss Sergei's case. At this meeting, he no longer opposed the court because his will was gone. Sometime after this court session, guards with black hoods over their faces beat him with a rubber hose that had metal inside it. After this, one good guard asked, "Is that you, Sergei?" Sergei replied, "Yes." As he shared this part of his story, tears flowed down his face. A short time later, the guards noticed Sergei, who was allowed to walk around outside with his shirt off, did not have any blue marks from the beatings or any tattoos, so at 9 a.m., Sergei went before the administrator. This man he looked at him, acted very surprised by the lack of marks and just walked around Sergei shrugging his shoulders.

These events were a precursor to better conditions for Sergei within the prison. Within his cell was a man named Ruslan; he was a leader in the cell. Ruslan knew Sergei, so he told someone among the guards that he was not to be touched. Time passed and life in prison seemed to improve. Sergei was put into another cell with better conditions and no one touched him anymore. He was even given a separate bed.

Throughout Sergei's time in prison, he was brought to court 40 times. Each time the court ordered him to appear, it discussed his situation, then stopped and waited a month; this foolishness continued for years. He never knew when the judge would decide his case. He also had trouble remembering how long he waited between court appearances. No matter the time, he continued going to a higher court and they continued to put him off. The court's goal was to wear him down like a weak animal until he had no more will or fight left in him. This harsh strategy was built into the system because there was no trust in the hearts of the officials and they were convinced that all of the prisoners were liars that must not receive any mercy. These events took place over three and one half years; they still made him wait one more year.

Finally, the Supreme Court ruled he was innocent; however, he was still labeled as a mercenary, or the person who was hired to commit the crime. He never received a document stating he was guilty. He now owed a lot of money to his lawyer, so he sold his car and paid a large amount of money to the lawyer and the court. Just before Sergei left the prison, he heard that the rich executive had been shot and killed. He also learned this man had paid a lot of money to the guards to beat and kill him. In addition, the executive paid substantial amounts of money to the lawyers and police to keep him in prison.

Despite these negative events, Sergei did not experience major problems while in prison because he had a very strong faith in God. He often appealed to the Lord and God showed Himself in unique and real ways. Near the end of his time in prison, he was given his own key to a separate study where no one would bother him. In the end, he was the only prisoner set free from his cell. Ultimately, Sergei spent eight and one half years in prison. Our interview ended with this question, "Sergei, how did you feel when your wife and four children met you at the prison gate upon your release?" Weeping, he said, "It was like heaven."

Mehaill Porhornovich Strelkov

Upon entering the small home of Mehaill and Lidia Porhornovich Strelkov, I met a sweet and loving couple that knew Jesus as their personal Savior. During their lives, they weathered many storms and came out victorious. Mike was raised by his parents and had three siblings. In Lidia's family, there were seven children. Mehaill and Lidia have one son who lives in Novosibirsk with his five children and a son in Germany who has one son and one daughter.

Mehaill Porhornovich Strelkov, also known as Mike, lived with his family in the Ukraine during the 1930's when life was very difficult. The Russian government offered free land to individuals who came to Siberia to make their living. Therefore, Mike's parents moved the family of to a village about 150 kilometers south of Tomsk, which is four and one half hours north of Novosibirsk, to work on a collective farm.

Life on the farm was very difficult because the farm's director was very strict. The residents of the farm had to work every day of the year from sun up until sun down. If someone did not work, he was sent to prison. Temperatures were negative 30 to negative 50 degrees. Numerous people froze to death and even the birds that flew searching for food fell to the ground frozen. Family members shared only one pair of boots amongst one another and clothing was very inadequate. In addition, the children had to walk to school in this extreme cold.

If residents of the collective farm wanted to go into town to sell products from their farms, the director had to give them a document. With the very small amount of money they earned, they purchased salt, sugar, matches and pepper.

In addition to the little income the family was able to make, the government required a daily tax. Each family gave the authorities between 250 and 300 liters of milk. They were also required to give edible items such as eggs and meat. If the required amount of the government's tax was short, they demanded more from the people; this was a way to show their support of the war. If the family had any milk or products left over, they could use them. Fortunately, Mike's family had a cow that produced a lot of milk. One day the cow bore a calf. Mike's mother killed the one-month-old calf and hid it under the bed. When the inspector came to ask about the calf, they told him it ran away. Later, Mike's family enjoyed the young calf's meat for themselves.

In 1942, Mike's father left to fight in the war; he did not return and the family never knew what happened to him. When Mike was older, he also enrolled in the army. Upon his return from the war, obtained a passport and moved to Novosibirsk. Documents were, and still are, very important in Russia; everything is documented with some kind of a document.

Maria at the Razavet Church

In 1948, in the city of Novosibirsk, many believers who were both men and women, worked at a factory that made secret weapons. During their lunch breaks, they met together and studied God's word. The factory leaders told the group to stop meeting, but instead, the group told the leaders the stones would cry out if they were silent. After this, the group was not persecuted for their faith; however, the authorities influenced the minds of the people that worked in the factory. (Ultimately, the believers who met together were sent to prison for 10 years.)

At that same time, Maria was encouraged to join these meetings; however, she could not because her work required she stay at her post. She controlled the product that was under high temperatures and the process required constant monitoring. After she declined the invitation, some believers from Prokopievsk joined the fellowship luncheons. One day, one of these men got some foreign matter in his eye and had to go to the hospital. After this man was released, he and some other men went to Maria's house. The injured man asked for Maria's hand in marriage, but she refused because she did not know if he was a good man.

Maria wanted to quit her job at the factory; however, the director told her she would go to prison the day she quit and got married. You see, the factory leaders thought she wanted to marry this young man, but all of the leaders were informers and POW's from the war. She would not have married any of these leaders because of her Christian values.

Maria not only had a strong value system, she was compassionate. One day she and her friend visited a man who injured his arms and legs while fighting in WWII. As the man's health improved, so did his desire to get married. He prayed a long time about marrying Maria. He even told her he saw her in a white wedding gown. Maria was confused because she thought it would not be right to marry an invalid. Three years later, he asked for Maria's hand in marriage. Her mother said she would have to earn the money for both of them for the rest of their lives. Maria agreed to the proposal, married in 1950 and registered the marriage license. Her husband was now Isaiah Govelovich Voitov.

One month after she married, she had to report to the NKVD (*Black Raven*) office. The officials informed her that it was not right for her to marry an invalid since she worked in a secret factory. The officials wanted her to change jobs, but she said she had not committed any crime because the constitution gave the right to religious freedom. Maria was also told that if she must pray, then pray at home; she told them she could not live without the fellowship of other believers. The officials then tried to frighten her by threatening to send her to prison, even though she was married to an invalid, which was illegal. At that time, the law forbade a spouse to be sent to prison if the other spouse was an invalid. The officials told Maria she could not continue to attend church or go to choir practice. When the NKVD (*Black Raven*) asked her who sang in the choir, she told them that anyone could sing if they desired to do so. She gave them no names even though they kept asking.

The official's probing continued. They asked her about the choir and how many people were in it. Then they pulled out a list and told her the names of the choir members. By that point, she did not know if she had betrayed any of the members. Her questioning began at 9 a.m. and ended around 7 p.m. The officials even changed shifts as they tried to wear her down. No matter how much the men probed, Maria remained steadfast. Their whole purpose was to change her mind about God.

After the questioning by the NKVD (*Black Raven*), she returned to the factory where they tried to get her to change her mind about God again. During her five-minute breaks, the factory leader talked with her about changing her mind. She did not witness in the factory because the oppressors were told that Baptists were dangerous. However, she did not deny her faith either. Maria explained that over the past 13 years, between 1951 and 1964, she had been giving birth to their children. This is when the factory leaders interrogated Isaiah. He told the leaders he stayed home and watched the children. They then wanted to know why they had so many children. Maria told them it was a sin for believers to abort babies. Throughout this questioning, the leaders attempted to get Isaiah and Maria to say different things. Fortunately, God protected them and gave them the right answers every single time. He also kept others from lying about them.

The lives of both Maria and Isaiah were very busy. Because of this, she did not attend church all of the time. Therefore, her husband listened to programs on the radio, wrote down poems and gave them to her. When Maria was at church, she always had something fresh to quote; this was very encouraging to all of the believers. Sometimes her husband kept the children, cooked the food and shopped while she washed the clothes.

One day, the factory workers were told to go to a cultural club to improve themselves. The leaders said this act would cause the workers to produce more. Maria told them she did not have an opportunity to attend the cultural club. That was when they reminded her that she had time to go to church. She countered their fact and said that worship at church gave her peace and comfort and did not cost anything. The factory interrogators then told Maria that the factory was like a big family and needed the money. In addition, after she attended the theater, she would be considered a good worker. Maria did not obey this request, so she did not receive her bonus.

Later in life, Maria retired from the factory and attended the Salvation Baptist Church in Novosibirsk. It was here that Brother Edvard Aldophovich Jenrick encouraged her to share her poems. Because she did not, she was blind for two weeks; she could not even see a spoon on the table. Maria knew God had made her eyesight go away. In response to God, she said, "Praise God; I will not be silent anymore." That was when she began to write poems herself, but humbly said she did not want to promote herself in anyway. For 66 years, Maria wrote poems; she still has her entire collection today.

Sometime in 1993, a neighbor told Maria about an eye center where she could get an operation to restore her eyesight. Therefore, her daughter-in-law took her to the eye center and one eye was restored. The operation cost 46,000 rubles in old money, or about one half of a month's salary, which was far too much for her salary. Later, the law changed which made the surgery free for retired people. Maria had a second surgery in 1994. This time insurance paid 10,000 rubles, the factory paid 20,000 and she paid the remaining 16,000.

She now continues serving God with the gifts He has given her. At the time of our interview, Maria was 81 years old and had 21 grandchildren and four great-grandchildren. Throughout life, Maria and her family lived with God's help. They could not rely on the government, but they could rely on God and He never abandoned them. Maria was a wonderful woman who will tell her story until her last breathe.

Stalin's Spy

Vera's father was an officer who trained troops for the front line in the war. His troops were not afraid of anything. If a soldier lagged behind, he was shot by one of his own men. Her father let his tired, young soldiers rest and gave them a good book to read. Afterwards, they were ready to fight again. The troops went into battle shouting for Stalin and for the motherland and died with Stalin on their lips.

At one point, his left hand was wounded and he was hospitalized for some time. He was later reassigned and taught politics to the troops. By the end of his career in the military, Vera's father was a general who led his troops very well. Vera's uncle was also enlisted in the army and served as a doctor. One day he suddenly had a stomach problem, so he went to the bushes to relieve himself. While there, a bomb hit the troops and everyone was killed except him.

While in Tomsk, Vera's father met a girl. Three days later, they were married; in total, they celebrated 62 years together. Both of Vera's parents thought Stalin was a great man, so sometime during their marriage, Vera's mother, Annya, agreed to go to Germany as a spy for Stalin. She wore the swastika, but sent messages back to the Kremlin. At one time, she and Stalin's right-hand man told Stalin they could take Hitler. Stalin responded by saying that in Germany, there was an Armenian, high-ranking officer who would take over the leadership of Germany and Stalin might loose the war. As a result, Stalin refused to let them touch Hitler. On another occasion, Annya sent word to Stalin, through his assistant, that Hitler was going to attack Russia on June 22, 1941; Stalin refused to believe it because earlier he had signed a peace-pack with Hitler. The war clouds had been gathering for some months in Germany and on June 22, 1941 Adolph Hitler launched his swift attack on Russia. Poland had already succumbed to the German military machine and now Moscow was being threatened. The German army came within twelve miles west of Moscow and the cold winter weather saved Moscow at this time from being overrun by the German tanks. The weather was so cold that the German tanks had difficulty moving. The grease in the wheels did not want to allow movement of the tank tracks.

Nadezhda and her Family

Nadezhda was born during the late 1950's in the city of Mariupol, which is located in eastern Ukraine. She grew up in a Christian family that worshiped in the city's underground Pentecostal church. The church met at five or six o'clock in the morning, before most people awoke. Its members tried to deflect suspicion, so they walked in twos or threes to the church meetings.

If the NKVD (*Black Raven*) came to the church meeting, the church sisters made a circle with an opening as a way for the church brothers to escape. Nadezhda's grandmother served as a deacon in the church, and helped the families after their loved ones returned from the prison camps. Often, when the men returned, they had lice in their hair, so she helped them clean up and get rid of the lice. She also provided food and clothing for the men. Nadezhda spent a lot of time helping with her grandmother. In addition, she gained a lot of wisdom and experience as she and her grandmother asked God about how to help those needy people.

Within the city of Mariupol, the police had a rule stating if someone's name was given five times because of worshiping, the individual went to prison. When a man was arrested, he spent between 8 and 12 years in prison. Nadezhda's family knew the day would come when their father would be arrested, so they taught their children to be ready. They also kept a pair of warm socks and bread ready for when their father's turn came.

The day finally came in 1964 when the KGB (*Black Raven*) knocked on their window. Nadezhda's sister and her father were in the kitchen cooking breakfast. Nadezhda ran to her father and he held her very closely. She said, "Papa, do not give me away." He replied, "You know the living God, and just as He did not leave me in the war, neither will He leave you. Keep everything we have taught you and be faithful until death. If we don't get to see each other again in this world, we will meet in heaven." When he finished he said, "I love you very much." Nadezhda's older sister was now very afraid as she realized the authorities were going to take their father. As the police took him away, Nadezhda cried and tried to get close to her father, however, the police threw her from him. They handcuffed him and read a false statement.

While the arrest occurred, Nadezhda's mother was at work. This meant the children would be at home alone. The police would not allow this, so they took everyone who was in the house. The men lured the children into their car by saying they would be taken to their mother. Her father kept saying, "Hold on to Jesus; He will not leave you and now is the time to apply all I taught you.

Believe and be willing to suffer just as the preachers preached."

The police never took the children to their mother. Instead, they were taken to an internat school, run by the government. Upon their arrival, the headmaster said, "You are in a good place now, so be good Soviet girls and forget about your God." Nevertheless, Nadezhda said in her heart that she would never, ever forget her God. The children were given new clothes and then put into the children's home. The school's leaders told the children that they no longer had a father or mother and the government would now provide everything for them. After this, Nadezhda's only desire was to be alone so she could pour out her heart to God through prayer and ask for strength. She also quickly realized the most terrible thing that could happen was for her to deny Jesus.

Because there were constantly so many girls and teachers around, there was no place for her to be alone. Therefore, she decided to just kneel down and pray right there in the classroom; she did not care what the school leaders would do to her. Children teased her and tickled her, but through her prayer, she flew away in her heart. Nadezhda prayed for herself, her parents and her sister who was in another class. Once she realized someone was shaking her, she opened her eyes and saw the angry headmaster woman who asked, "What are you doing?" In a rage, that woman pulled her pigtails, but Nadezhda did not feel any pain. The headmaster then took her to a dark storage room in the basement. As Nadezhda felt around, her eyes tried to adjust to the darkness. It was then that she touched something and it fell to the floor. She was now happy to be alone because she could pray and sing to her God. After some time, she fell asleep. She awoke when she heard something scratching; she realized it was rats. Because she was afraid they would bite her, she prayed and asked God for help. Nadezhda then turned to the corner so she would not see them. Just then, the door opened and she was taken back to the classroom where she was mocked and teased. Even though she was just persecuted, she was happy because she counted it a privilege to suffer for Jesus.

Throughout Nadezhda's time at the school, the teachers told many lies about the Christians. They said they sacrificed children to their God and that the children were bound when they came to arrest the father. The teachers also claimed they rescued the children from their parents and brought them to this school. Nadezhda knew this was not true and said, "My father loves me and I love him." In response, the teachers asked, "Who were the ones preaching in your church, and who was in your house? Who did you baptize, and who baptized you? Who were the guests in your house?" Nadezhda told them, "Who normally tells who had guests in their home?" That discussion continued five times a day because they wanted her to betray her people. Nadezhda tired of this questioning and wanted to cry, but knew that if she did, the victory would go to Satan; so she did not cry.

At one point, she was placed in a room with eight other girls; she told them she was a Christian. She also told the girls how much she liked to sing and pray to Jesus. One girl said, "Talk quieter because someone may be listening at the door." Therefore, Nadezhda whispered and asked if anyone wanted to become a Christian. She also said, "Tomorrow you may go to hell if you don't repent now." Because Nadezhda believed Jesus was coming soon, she talked to the girls like this for a week. In time, one of the girls told the headmaster about Nadezhda's actions and she was again put into the basement with the rats. The headmaster told Nadezhda, "If you don't stop telling people about your God, this basement will become your permanent bedroom!" Nadezhda knew her actions had to continue because others in the Bible also suffered for Jesus. During her time in the basement, she cried a lot and ate very little. When the headmaster took her to breakfast, she could not eat. She had no appetite because she had remembered the wonderful times of worship and how her mother had cooked pies for the family.

One morning there were many sweets set on the table; she knew it was difficult to obtain sweets during that time. The teachers asked if she liked all of these things and said the sweets were for her. They also said, "You can have these every day if you will deny Jesus." She stopped eating, jumped up, ran to her room and closed the door because she was afraid she had denied her Lord. Nadezhda told the Lord that the teachers had lied to her. As she continued to pray, she remembered that her mother had taught her that God knows our hearts and He sees our motives.

For the next three months, she was not allowed to go on the street by herself. Therefore, the headmaster, or a teacher, tied a rope to her wrist and held onto her as they strolled outside; they were afraid she would run away. Nadezhda missed her family so much, so she prayed and asked God to bring her back to her family. She desperately wanted to return to her parents and the other brothers and sisters in their church.

One day, while she stood at the window praying silently, she tried to recall all of the Bible verses she had been taught because she did not have a Bible. Nadezhda remembered that God said, "I know the thoughts and desires that I have for you, and how to lead you." Just then, she heard a girl crying, so she walked down stairs and saw her father. Nadezhda could not believe her eyes. Her father had not been put into prison because he was not a preacher. Her 18-month stay in the orphanage had just ended.

While Nadezhda and her sister were separated from their parents, her father and mother had gone to Kiev and Moscow to obtain documents for their release. Because her father showed his medals from the war, there were no arguments. When she saw her father, it was the happiest moment of her life except for her relationship with Jesus Christ.

At the age of 13, Nadezhda went to the orphanage again. This time it was for only six months. She believes God wanted to test her heart and love for Him again.

Maria Zaharchenko in Mariupol

Feuder, Maria Zaharchenko's second husband, greeted me at the gate of their home in Mariupol. After a brief handshake, he pulled me close, and I attempted to give him my left cheek; he refused. I then gave him my right cheek; he refused that too. I thought, "I' am going to have to let this man kiss me, or I will not be able to meet Maria and take this interview." You guessed it; he planted one right on the smackers.

After introductions, we settled in for our interview. I found Maria, as I am sure you will too, to be a strong Ukrainian woman who endured a very hard life. World War II started on June 22, 1941, and in September of that year, the Germans invaded Russia. At the time, none of the churches in Russia were open and many people were in prison. In addition, no one was allowed to talk about God, and if a Bible was found in someone's home, that individual went to prison for 10 years.

It was when the German Army was within a number of kilometers of Moscow, that Stalin allowed the churches to open for prayer for the motherland. That was when the believers that had been in hiding came out and started to gather for prayer. This was also when both the Orthodox and Baptists met in separate places for prayer and worship.

One day, Maria's neighbor told her sister Luba that she was attending a church, but it did not have any flowers for decoration. Luba went to the garden, picked some flowers and brought them back to their neighbor. Then the neighbor asked Luba if she wanted to come to the service. Since Luba had no clothes to wear, she said she could not go out. Maria overheard the conversation and wanted to attend the service; Luba was delighted. Therefore, both Maria and Luba quickly got ready and went to church with their neighbor. To their dismay, very few people were there.

Time passed and Maria was presented with additional opportunities to attend church. A Baptist family, which consisted of only the oldest son and the parents, also lived in Mariupol asked Maria to attend church with them many, many times. Unfortunately, she did not understand anything that was said in the services, even though many young people played instruments and prayed. Maria would kneel and close her eyes to pray with the people, but she understood nothing because her mind and heart were closed to accepting the information; however, she did have a desire to attend.

Within one or two months, the weather turned cold; so Maria and Luba went to the Pentecostal church just three kilometers away. They noticed the people in this church prayed in another language. The first preacher read some verses, and so did the second; however,

Maria still did not understand. But by the time the last preacher read about Jesus on the cross, and how He prayed "Father forgive them for they do not understand what they are doing," she very clearly understood. It was in that very moment everything became clear; it was as if a veil had been removed from her eyes and she could see what the gospel was all about. Something also touched her and caused her to sob and pray to God. She said it felt very good, and yet she did not know why. Maria also prayed within her heart, "God, I will always come here and stay here." That became her promise to God; and on that day, God was the only one who knew she wanted to serve Him. Maria does not remember exactly how old she was. She guessed she was probably 15 years old, but she did know it was June 26; she continues to attend that church today.

During wartimes, no one freely attended church because of the guards on the streets. However, when the guards were not there, the people would sneak out to go to church. These guards were very strict and would not permit anything that pertained to Christianity. Therefore, there were no Bibles. Because of this, Maria listened to every word spoken in church; she was blessed to have a very good memory. She had a great desire to attend church, but seldom went due to the soldiers. On February 19, 1946, she was sent to Eastern Germany for three years. The government sent her there to work in a weapons factory.

There were no churches in Germany; however, she had God's word in her heart, the same words she heard while at her church in Russia. She also prayed a lot because no one was allowed to write letters to loved ones back home. Just three years after her arrival in Germany, she was given back her freedom and returned home at the beginning of March. On April 20, 1946, Pastor Ledemyanovich baptized her in the sea.

Sometime during the early part of May 1949, while she prayed with her uncle, cousin and sister-in-law, she heard God speak to her. The Lord said, "Daughter, prepare your heart because something very hard is coming, and you will be tested severely. And through those hard times, you will remember the trials of Job. He was a very righteous man and was tested greatly, and so will you face many, many difficulties, but I will guide you through it." She did not know what God planned for her, but trusted He would take care of her. Later that year, Maria had a church wedding where she wed a man, Volodya, who was a preacher and member of the church. She and her husband had two good years together; unfortunately, eight very difficult years followed because Volodya gradually stopped following God and attending church. From the time she heard the Lord's words, until he left her, it was 13 years.

After Volodya fell from God, and recanted his faith, he became very abusive and made her life very rough. She became afraid of him because he frequently beat her and totally controlled her life. Nothing she did pleased him and he did not approve of anything she did. Their children were small during this time, and saw what happened to their mother. Maria prayed often during these persecutions and asked for God's strength. It was now very seldom that she attended church, primarily because of Volodya's persecution, but also because of the guards. Her husband did not allow her to pray at home, and one day he said, "If you pray in this house again, I will chop your head off with the hatchet." From then on, she prayed outside in the garden, and never again in the house.

She bore her first child, and when their second son Zenia was born, she wanted to pray with her husband before they went to the hospital; he refused. Maria eventually learned her Volodya had denounced God because the NKVD (*Black Raven*) had scared him. They said that if he did not recant his faith he would go to prison for a long time. This denunciation meant she would be alone in following God; she could not lean on a Christian husband to help her fight the battles of life under communism and would not have help raising their seven children. His opposition to his faith was fierce; however, it was too small to cause Maria to denounce her faith in God.

Then the day came when Volodya said he would take the children and leave if she did not recant her faith. He told her she had three days to think about it; however, she told him she did not need three days. Her answer was that even though she knew it would be very hard, she would never ever leave God. Her husband told her she would loose her rights as a mother because he would take away their children. Volodya also said she would loose her faith because she could not live without her children, and then asked, "Do you know how to live without your children?" Maria said, "No. I know it will be hard, but God will help me. I will stay with God to the end, even if it means death." She knew these could only be the words of the Holy Spirit, and continued with, "God will strengthen me and I will be able to bear it." Her husband tried to make her see that the children would live in a different world. After that argument, he left with his mistress.

Maria now fought for God as the most important thing in her life. She said, "I have no strength, but God is strong." Maria's husband continued to find ways to get her to denounce her faith. He even went to the government and told them Maria was a Baptist. Volodya felt this would cause her to denounce her faith because he had helped a judge build his house; and now this judge would help him with his domestic problem. On August 13, 1962, Maria was arrested and her husband took the children away to his parents home. They cried a lot when they found out they could not go back home. All of Maria's neighbors tried to calm the children down, but it was a very difficult task. Maria only knew that at one point, God put a protective armor around her because, even though the children were screaming, she did not shed a tear.

On September 1, Volodya came and said, "Give me the children's documents and house documents; you have 10 days left to live in this house." By now, Maria's children were the following ages: Tanya 13, Zenia 11, Sasha 9, Luba 8, Annya 6, Sergei 4 and Natasha 3. At first, the children lived with their father, but he took them all to his parent's house who were non-believers that always supported him. These grandparents also tried to turn the children against their mother by saying she only knew how to pray to God. They also said, "Your mother left you for her God, and now only your father can help you to be a person." Maria could no longer see her children, and eventually, they began to fear her.

One day, when Maria saw her children, she asked them, "Why are you doing this?" They replied, "Because of our grandparents." Sometimes Maria met her children on the street, and they put their hands into their pockets so she could not give them anything. She even said, "Lubictka (her very affectionate name for Luba) I want to give you some candy," but her daughter would not talk to her. Her children looked at her, but never said anything. She talked to them, and asked them why they would not talk to her, but they would do nothing because they had been told not to take anything from her or talk to her.

Eventually, Volodya married his mistress and they lived with Maria's children in their house. One day, her son Zenia ran away and said to his father, "I will not live with you, but with mother." Because of this, they took

Maria's children to an orphanage and locked Zenia in a room so he could not run away. At this orphanage was a communist teacher who beat Zenia's head against the wall and said, "I will beat God out of your head." In response, Zenia held his head in his hands and ran away crying. Zenia also said, "I have only one mother, and I will not leave her." His heart was still with his mother even though he could not see her. The teacher even told Zenia he would put him in a big bag and send him off somewhere. Zenia replied, "If you do that, I will make a hole in the bag." The children spent between two and four years in this orphanage.

By now, Maria had been released from prison and had no house, no job, no children, no husband and no money, so she became a beggar. She asked people to let her do little, menial tasks, such as cleaning, washing floors and painting, in exchange for a few rubles. She also went to Christian people and asked them for work. All of these believers let her in because they loved God; however, all they could do was pray for her and give her some small work. Eventually, she found a job in the kitchen of a nursery carrying heavy pots and pans. Her salary was 10 rubles per month, (which today would be equivalent to 40 cents); other workers at that time received approximately 100 rubles, or more, per month. In addition, because she was now an 'enemy of the people,' she was required to pay a fine and give alimony money to the government for her children.

Her income was very low, her work was very hard, she ate a poor diet that made her sick and tired and her legs hurt. On top of that, she learned her document was bad. She experienced many failed attempts to find decent work because of these things, and her bad document. Several times, Volodya got her fired from jobs because he told bad things about her. One time, when she worked in the department of personnel, her boss called her up and screamed at her, insulted her and then fired her. One female accountant that knew Maria had no home even tried to help her. The woman told the authorities Maria's children were taken from her and that she did not abandon them. Nevertheless, the attempt was useless.

Time passed, and during the rule of Chairman Brezhnev, between 1964 and 1966, Maria's husband took their children 5,000 miles away to VladiVostok. From there, they moved to Barnaul. Ultimately, the children lived in many different cities in Russia because Volodya was trying to hide them from Maria. No matter where the family lived, he attempted to raise them as atheists and planted many negative attitudes in their minds. Because of his actions, the children opposed Christians and God, and were too little to resist their father's negative influence. There was no one to explain to them the truth about everything, but God helped them to realize everything later. In one more attempt to control his children, Volodya took a girl from the orphanage because he feared his children might grow up and leave. He believed that if his children left, at least this girl would stay behind and take care of him and his new wife. This girl turned out to be a bad girl who ran away and did other bad things. Maria's children grew up, and one-by-one got married; however, they still opposed their mother. Maria tried to contact her children many times, but they never responded because their father poisoned their minds and said Maria only believed in God. It was through those disappointments, she heard God say, "Wait until your former husband dies, and I will reunite you with your family and return your children to you." He also said she would meet someone.

Frequently, people asked Maria if she had seen her children. She said, "I am staying faithful and I am waiting." Many years passed and there were numerous failed attempts by both Maria and her children to find one another. During those years, she never lost hope because she remembered God told her she would not die until she saw her children again. Eventually in 2004, after 42 years, Maria and her children were reunited.

All of her children cried tears of happiness when they first met their mother again. Unfortunately, Sergei was not present, and never had a chance to see his mother again, because he was killed in a car accident at the age of 11. The family never learned the whole truth about the accident. In addition, when he died, Maria did not know it had happened, but she felt it because she had bad dreams about him. Sasha also missed the family's reunion because no one knew where he was or anything about him. During this first meeting, it was very hard for the children to call Maria 'mother.' Their father had forced them to call her Maria Semenovna, and they had gotten used to that. Even in their letters to her, they wrote "Dear Maria Semenovna" instead of 'Dear mother.' After their initial meeting, one of Maria's sons started going to church with his children, and he said he really enjoyed it. Her children continue to keep in contact with her. Zenia now says his mother is the best. Tanya married a German in Russia and, in 1995, moved to Germany. Luba lives in Novorossiysk and Anna lives in Barnaul. All of Maria's children are married and they visit her each summer. Maria also rejoices because all of her children and grandchildren now go to church and pray.

Before Volodya died, on May 9, 1997, his second wife said to him, "Pray to God." His response was, "Never say that to me about God." Other people also asked him to pray, but he refused because his heart was closed; therefore, he died without praying to God. Upon his death, his wife sent telegrams to all Maria's children; however, none of them received the notice in time to attend the funeral. Over time, the children realized their father was a sinner and said, "What kind of a man was he when none of his children went to his funeral?"

In 2006, all of Maria's living children came again to see her with their own families. Her children brought clothes and many gifts for her. She said she had everything she needed, so she gave away many of the clothes to people in need, and because there were too many for her. Each month, Maria now gets 440 rubles and Feuder receives 400 rubles; together they receive 840 rubles per month. They say it is enough for them and have gotten used to this lifestyle. The couple is happy because they have clothes, boots and do not need anything else. In addition, because they live in the Ukraine, they only pay 25% of the cost of their utilities, water, rent and other needs; the government pays the remaining 75%. In addition, their house is very old, but it is sufficient. It was built in 1911, before the revolution, and Maria has lived in it for 40 years. She cared for the original owner, Stephan Kondratovich who also was a believer, for eight years. When he died, he left the house to her. It was then she finally received a place of her own. Maria said, when the winters come, they use an oven that burns both wood and coal. It takes approximately one ton of coal to heat the house during these cold months, but it only costs about 250 rubles. Both Maria and Feuder said, "We lead a very calm, happy life now."

I did not understand everything about Maria's story; however, I caught enough to know this dear saint of God had suffered in ways that defied description. You saw how Maria's strength came from God, and God alone. For a long time, her faith was tested by fire, but she came out victorious. She now enjoys life and seeing her children and grandchildren. Both Maria and Feuder enjoy their old house and their very productive garden that occupies Feuder's time.

If God tested you like he tested Maria, would you stay faithful until the end?

Vladimir Vilchinsky

Vladimir Vilchinsky and his family lived in Brest, (a city) located in southwest Belorussia. It was here that he pastored a Baptist church, and in 1967, he helped organize a public worship service to celebrate the 100th anniversary of Baptist presence in Russia. The event was disrupted when he was accused of illegally performing a Baptism and resisting authority.

One day following this celebration, 1,000 people gathered in a forest and had a private worship service. Despite their secrecy, the worshipers were very jubilant. A children's choir sang, an orchestra played and several pastors preached, including Brother Vladimir. Near the platform hung a large banner that read, *Remember the way which you were led by the Lord.*

Government authorities heard about this meeting and arrived in trucks just as the meeting began. Using three video cameras, six NKVD (*Black Raven*) officers and 15 military personnel recorded everything, and quietly sat by saying nothing. However, when one of the preachers mentioned the persecution that Baptists faced, the men were no longer silent. Through a bullhorn, one of them yelled, "I demand that you come to the truck at once."

For the next eight months, the NKVD (*Black Raven*) investigated Vladimir and his family. One officer even told Vladimir he was appalled that he would invite children to attend the worship service and that action would not be forgiven. He also said, "This is the end of your freedom." On April 15, 1968, after a three-day trial in the Russian court, Vladimir and his brother were sentenced to five years in prison.

Vladimir spent the first four months of his sentence in one cramped prison cell with 40 other men. He said, "The prison for robbers, murderers and rapists was more like a gutter than a prison cell." A small slit in the ceiling provided a little bit of outside light while a single light bulb burned both day and night. The prisoners slept on a dirty, concrete floor and their toilet was a large bucket that sat in the corner of the cell. The air was horrible and the stench was enormously unbearable. Life was so miserable for the prisoners that they would write things on the walls in their own blood. One sign said, "Farewell life."

Vladimir was later released to a work camp and he was very thankful he could breathe in good clean air and talk to other inmates. When he was not working in the camp, he enjoyed talking with five other Christian men who encouraged one another. Many times Vladimir thought about Psalm 23. It reminded him that the Lord truly was his shepherd and that he did not have any wants beyond fellowshipping with his Lord. Prayer was forbidden in the prison, and one day when he bowed his head to pray, a guard snatched his food. Vladimir said, "This was a cruel joke, but very real just the same."

After his release in 1973, the government continued to persecute his family. Many, many times, other children called his children names; it was done in a merciless way that they had to endure. Sometime during 1974, his daughter, Galina, was imprisoned because she had worked in a Siberian camp for three years teaching the Bible to children. After five years in prison, she was released; and on November 19, 1979, less than three months later, she was arrested again. This time, the NKVD (*Black Raven*) framed her by planting drugs in her luggage while she waited for a delayed flight. She was arrested at the gate and accused of drug peddling.

Galina now had to wait in VladiVostok for her verdict. While she waited, her sister traveled 7,000 miles to visit her, but was not allowed. Many times the government dragged their feet when processing prisoners, so Galina stayed in the horrible prison Lvov for a year. The food was terrible and the conditions were harsh conditions; it all took a toll on her health. During that year, she lost eight teeth, much of her hair fell out and she became very emaciated and gaunt looking.

Finally, Galina was sentenced to three years and sent to a camp in Primorsky Krai. There were 2,000 women at this camp and they were all forced to work 10 hours per day and meet work quotas. During the winter, the barracks was unheated, and in the fall and spring, it was damp and cold. In order to survive, the women learned how to eat certain grasses and berries. However, no matter how bad the conditions were, Galina continually told the other women about her Jesus.

When her mother visited her, she was alarmed at how gaunt and decrepit she looked. Galina told her mother these words, "Momma, don't cry. I did not come here to sit on my hands. I am compelled by my Lord to speak to these perishing sinners about Christ. If I do not return, know then that I will die joyfully for Christ's sake. I am prepared to accept whatever God sends my way."

In 1982, the prison officials told Galina that she would suffer if she did not stop talking to the women about God. Later, word came out that the officials told a hardened inmate to beat Galina. This inmate, and another prisoner, beat Galina while two others held the door. Praise the Lord, in August of that same year, she finished her term and returned to her parents where they, and 500 friends, welcomed her home. The following verse describes her joy:

> When the Lord turned again the captivity of Zion, we were like them that dream. Then was our mouth filled with laughter, and our tongue with singing: then said they among the heathen, The Lord hath done great things for them. The Lord had done great things for us; whereof we are glad. – Psalm 126:1-3 (KJV).

Galina's health had been broken, but not her spirit. Russia's atheistic plan had failed to destroy her faith in God, but the authorities were not finished with her yet.

In October of that same year, the NKVD (*Black Raven*) summoned her, interrogated her and asked why she did not go to the registered church. Her response was, "I don't want to be unfaithful to Christ." The men responded by saying, "We will disgrace you before all Christians." The NKVD (*Black Raven*) required all churches to register with the government so they could control them. They chose the pastors and the sermon had to be pre-approved. In addition, children were forbidden to attend church services. Thank God, these requirements are no longer held for the churches in Russia.

In 1994, Vladimir's children encouraged him and his wife to join them in the United States of America. He does not consider America a reward for the suffering he experienced in Belorussia; he knows his real reward will come when he meets his Lord Jesus in heaven. Since he left Belorussia, there have been times when he has had nightmares about that time in his life; he does not plan to return because life in America is good.

Vladimir also praises the Lord that Galina is married and lives in Novokuznetsk, which is located in the southern part of Kemerovo County. It was only through God's great, abundant, unchanging, powerful, and sustaining grace that kept these two dear saints from giving up during those bitter situations. Vladimir and Galina are true heroes.

CONCLUSION

The Russian people who lived under the communist system were tested to the limit. Whenever they faced an impossible situation, they found a way to go around the problem and continue with their lives. One of their biggest challenges was the NKVD (Black Raven). The knock at the door after 2 a.m. meant the bread-earner would be taken to prison or put to death. In addition, the remaining family members were left with their own type of sentence. The mother and children were considered 'enemies of the people' and it became a daily struggle to find food, shelter and clothing.

When individuals had all of their possessions taken away and given to the collective farm, they did not resist; they simply started over. As one family in Belorussia was forced to leave a very wealthy, productive farm, they quietly went into exile. They simply took a few items of clothing and obeyed their captors. What caused them to accept such a harsh life and continue living in those horrible conditions? It was their faith in God. Through their struggles, their strength of character rose up and creativity flowed as God wrapped His arms around them and met all of their needs. "Make sure that your character is free from the love of money, being content with what you have; for He Himself has said, 'I will never desert you, nor will I ever forsake you'" Hebrews 13:5 (NASB).

It was through poetry and music that the Russian people found strength and encouragement against the intense bitterness and suffering. In the church, individuals wrote and spoke poems from memory as a way to express their deep feelings. Nothing goes deeper into a Russian's heart than a poem; and no one loves poetry more than the people of Russia. As for music, Russians especially love the accordion, even to this day.

Throughout this book, you learned Christians are not perfect. This was especially demonstrated in the story about the mother who allowed her oldest daughter to marry a young man with tuberculosis. When the family's husband/father was killed while fighting in World War II, finding food became a daily struggle. Because this young man provided food for the family, the mother kept his secret from her daughter, a secret that would ultimately and deeply affect the entire family. When the woman's daughter became pregnant and learned of her husband's illness, she aborted her little son. Never again was there forgiveness or communication between this mother and daughter. This mother had made a decision based upon that moment and did not realize the long-term problems she created for her family. Keeping a secret, even under bitter circumstances, can have devastating results, and yet, what would you have done in that situation? I am sure this mother considered the following verse as she struggled with her decisions. "For I was hungry and you gave Me food, I was thirsty and you gave Me something to drink, I was a stranger and you brought Me together with yourselves and welcomed and entertained and lodged Me" Matthew 25:35 (AMP).

Even after a measure of freedom came to Russia in the early 1990's, the old system of government returned. One completely innocent man was arrested and kept in prison in Novosibirsk for eight years. He and the other prisoners were forced to live in the basement of the prison where fog from cigarette smoke permeated the air. It was only because God supernaturally protected his health that he was able to survive. He was strengthened daily by God's great grace and his fellowship with God plunged to depths he never imagined were possible. "And endurance (fortitude) develops maturity of character (approved faith and tried integrity). And character [of this sort] produces [the habit of] joyful and confident hope of eternal salvation." Romans 5:4 (AMP).

What can we learn from those who suffered so much at the hands of murderers? As a nation, I believe we too will suffer if we do not return to God. Both Stalin and Hitler slowly gained full authority to carry out their evil regimes. It was tragic that the common people did not see what was coming and put a stop to such totalitarianism. Evil men ruled, and the people suffered greatly at their hands. When even children are afraid to play with one another on the streets, one should take note that life is very unbalanced. As our government continues to gain more control over our daily lives, will we have the courage to recognize it and do something about it?

Every government that has given in to one man who claimed to be their savior has suffered at that man's hands. It is very true that power corrupts, and total power corrupts absolutely. I fear that much pain and suffering is just around the corner if America does not wake up and return to its spiritual roots. When good men rule, there is peace, when evil men rule, suffering follows. I pray Americans will wake up and return to God. I leave you with one last thought. "Doing what is right lifts people up. But sin brings shame to any nation." Proverbs 14:34 (NIRV).

Author and Grandson Graham
Photo by Kameron Bayne Images

Made in the USA